FAIRY TAILS 2

A GALLERY GIRLS COLLECTION

BRIAN LEBLANC '06

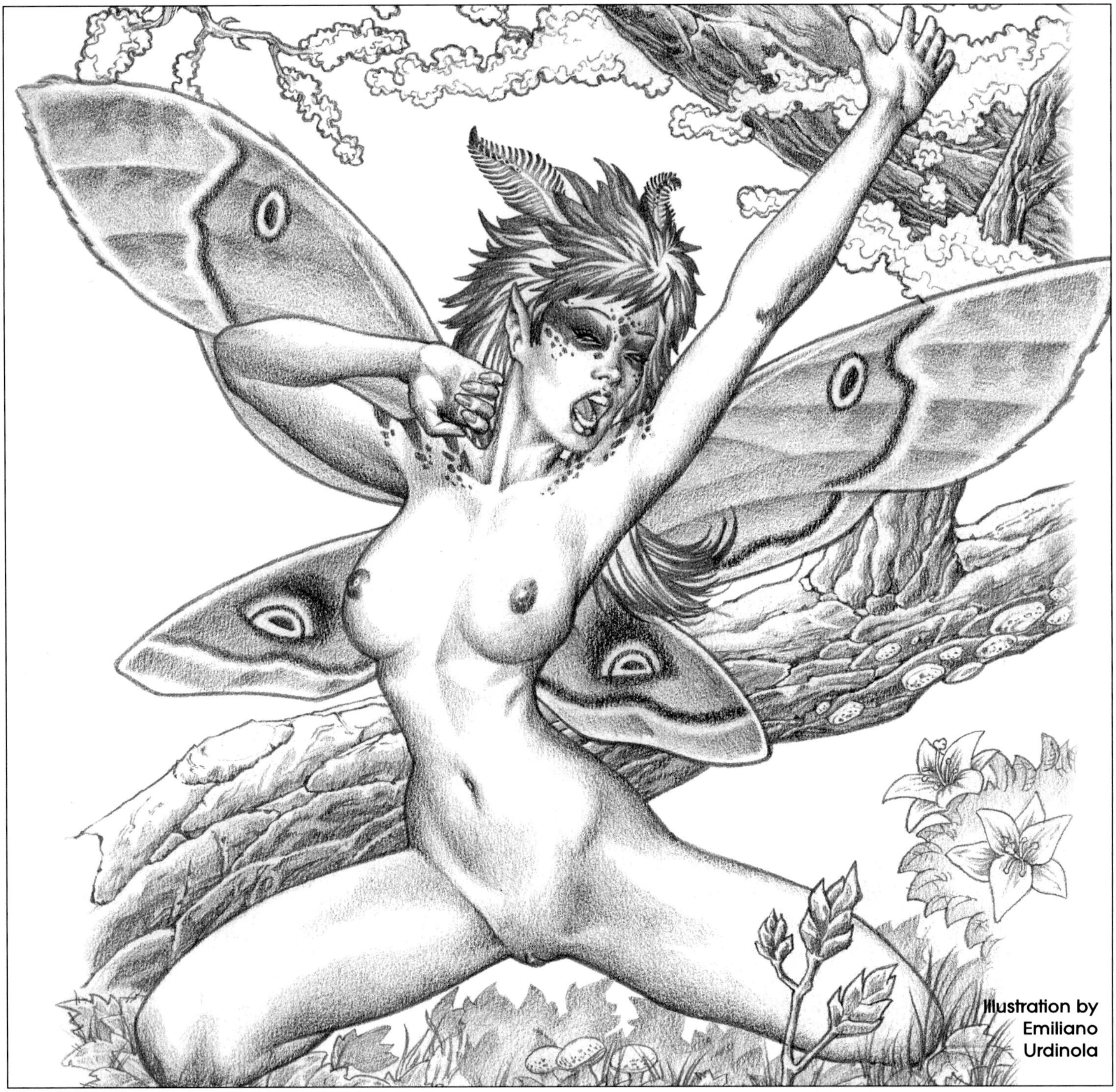

Illustration by
Emiliano
Urdinola

FAIRY TAILS

Volume Two

Book design by Grassy Knoll Studios.

Published by
SQP Inc.
PO Box 248 - Columbus, NJ 08022

Sal Quartuccio & Bob Keenan - Publishers

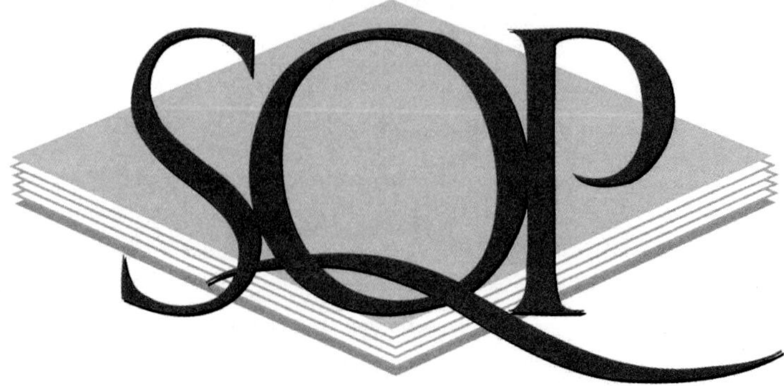

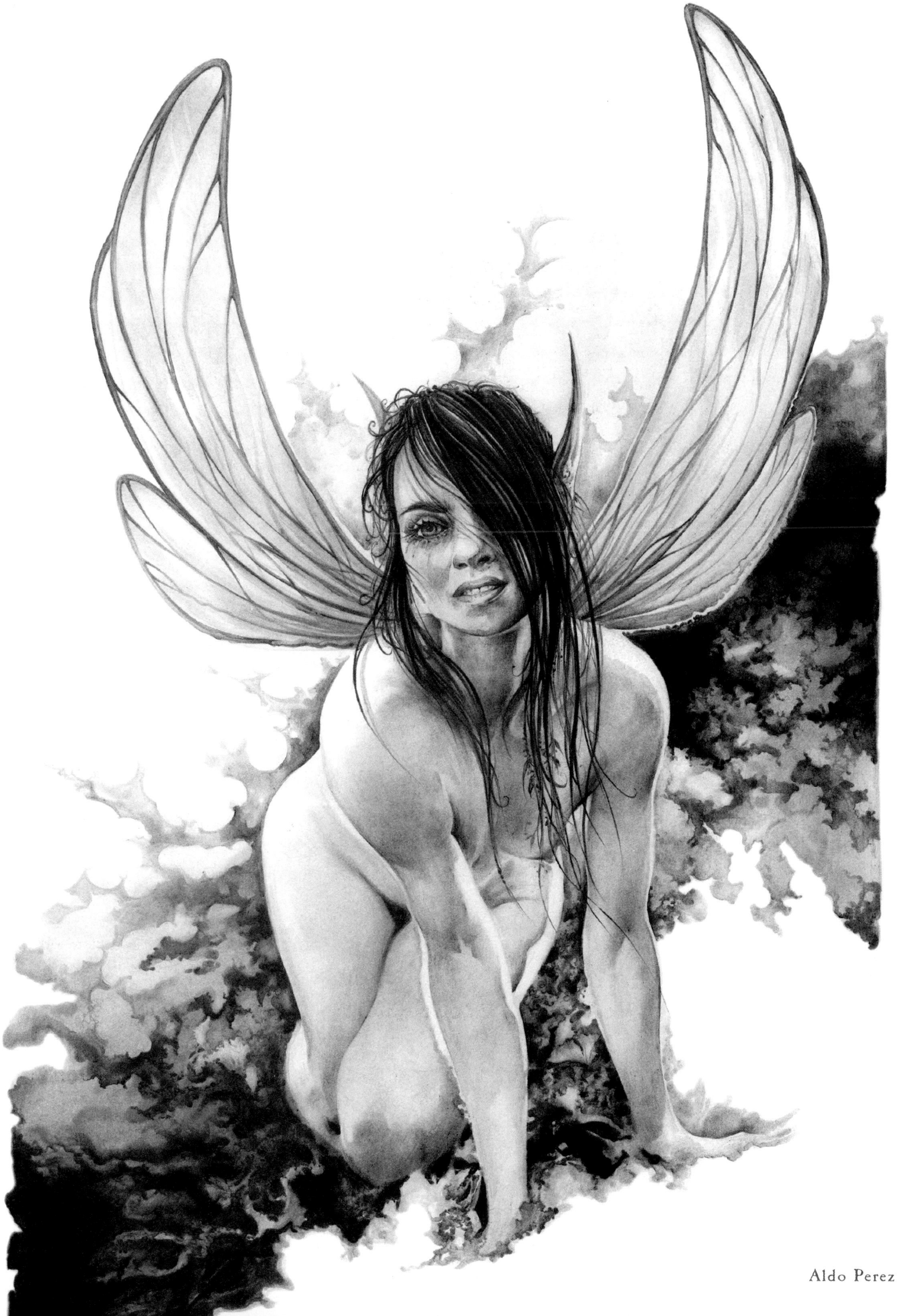

Aldo Perez

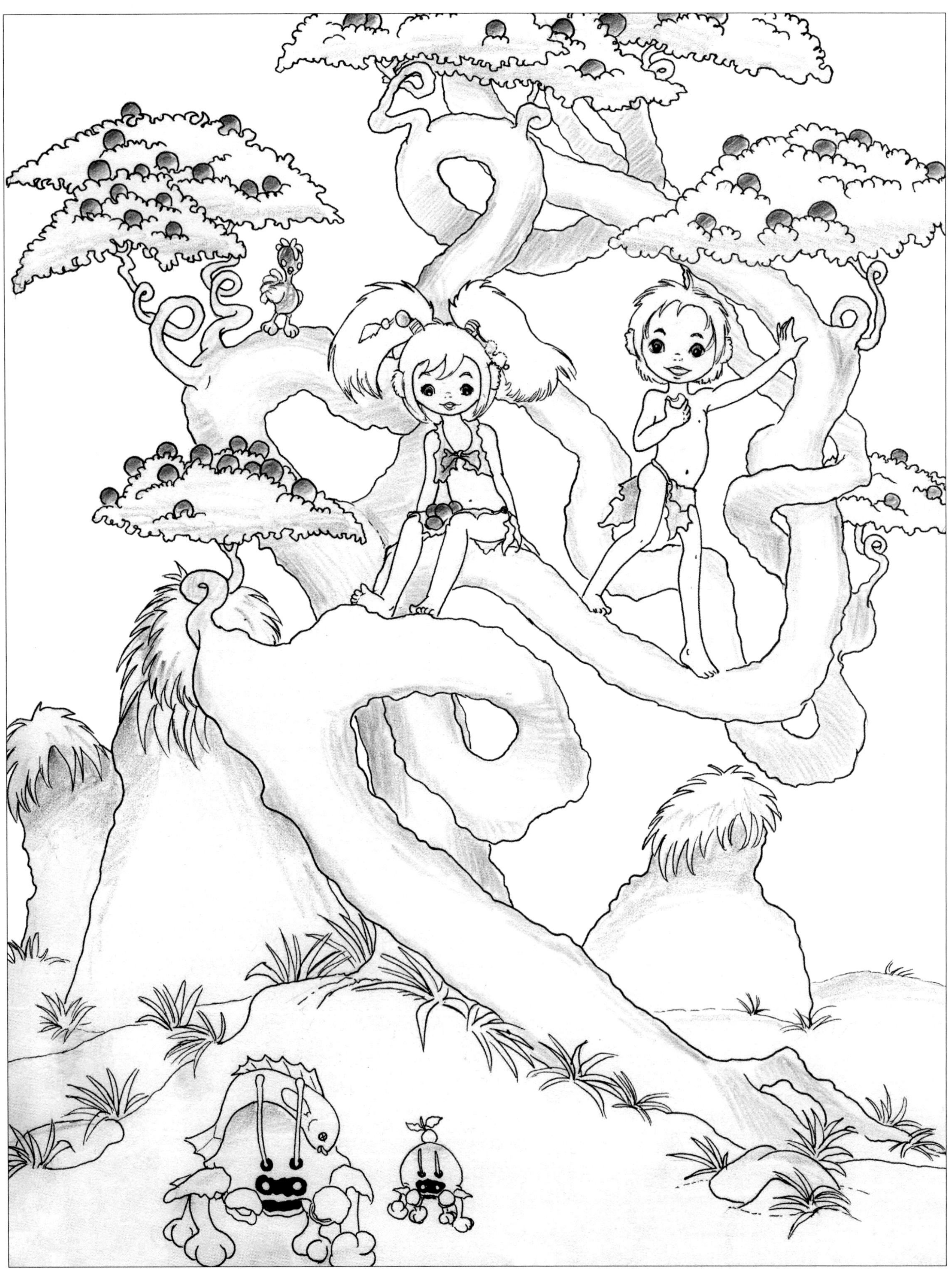

Barry Blair

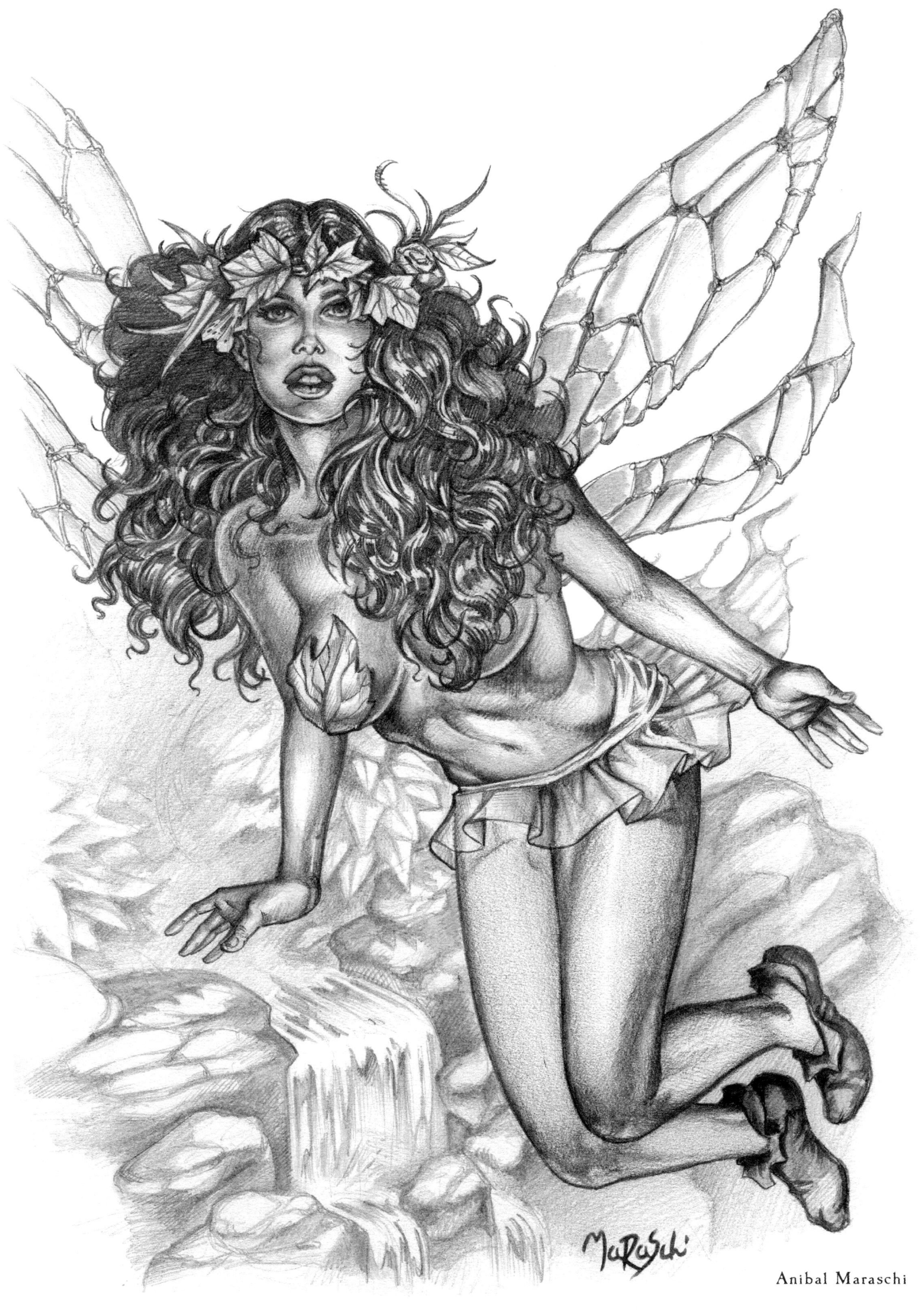

Anibal Maraschi

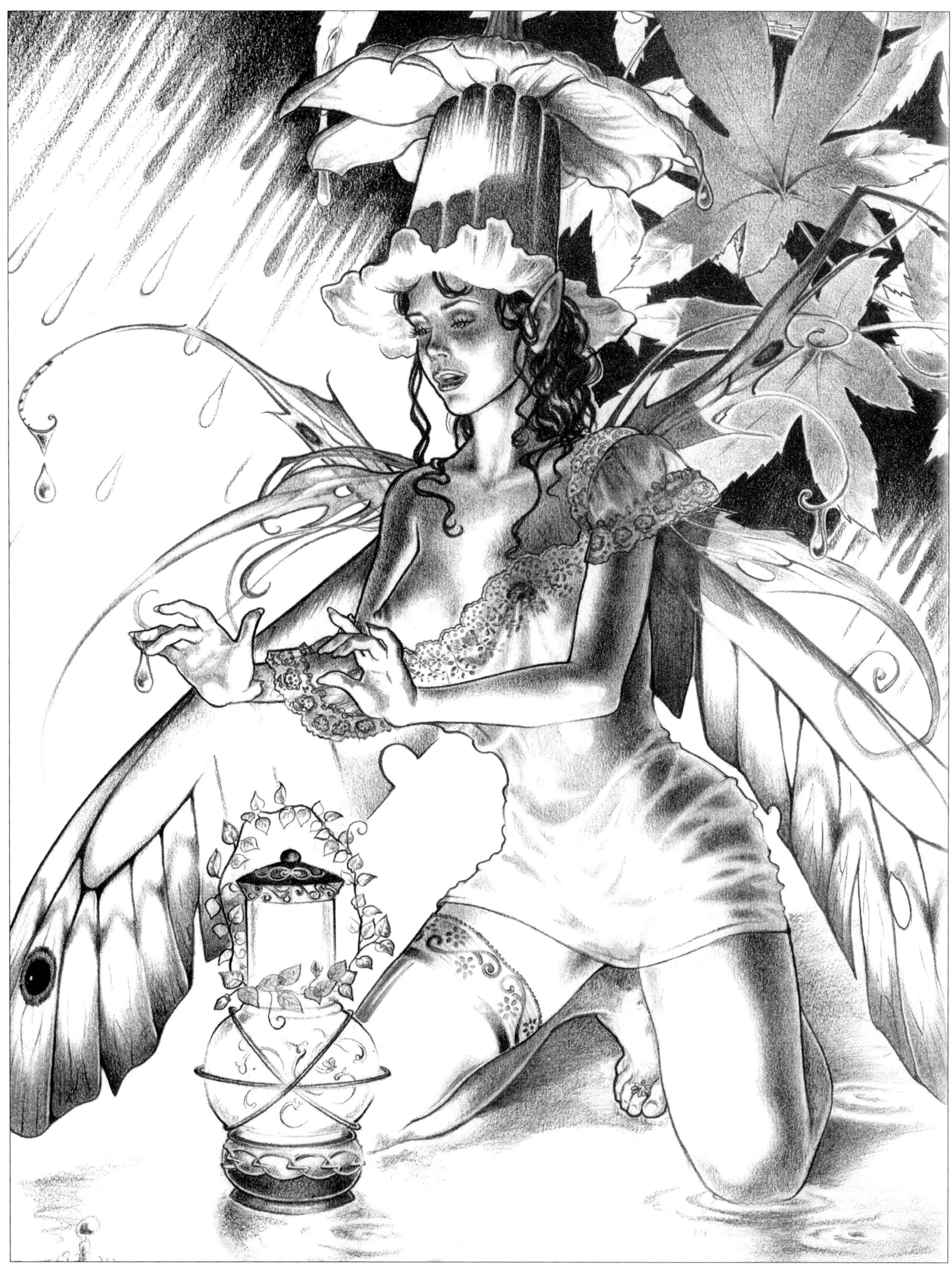

Perla Pilucki

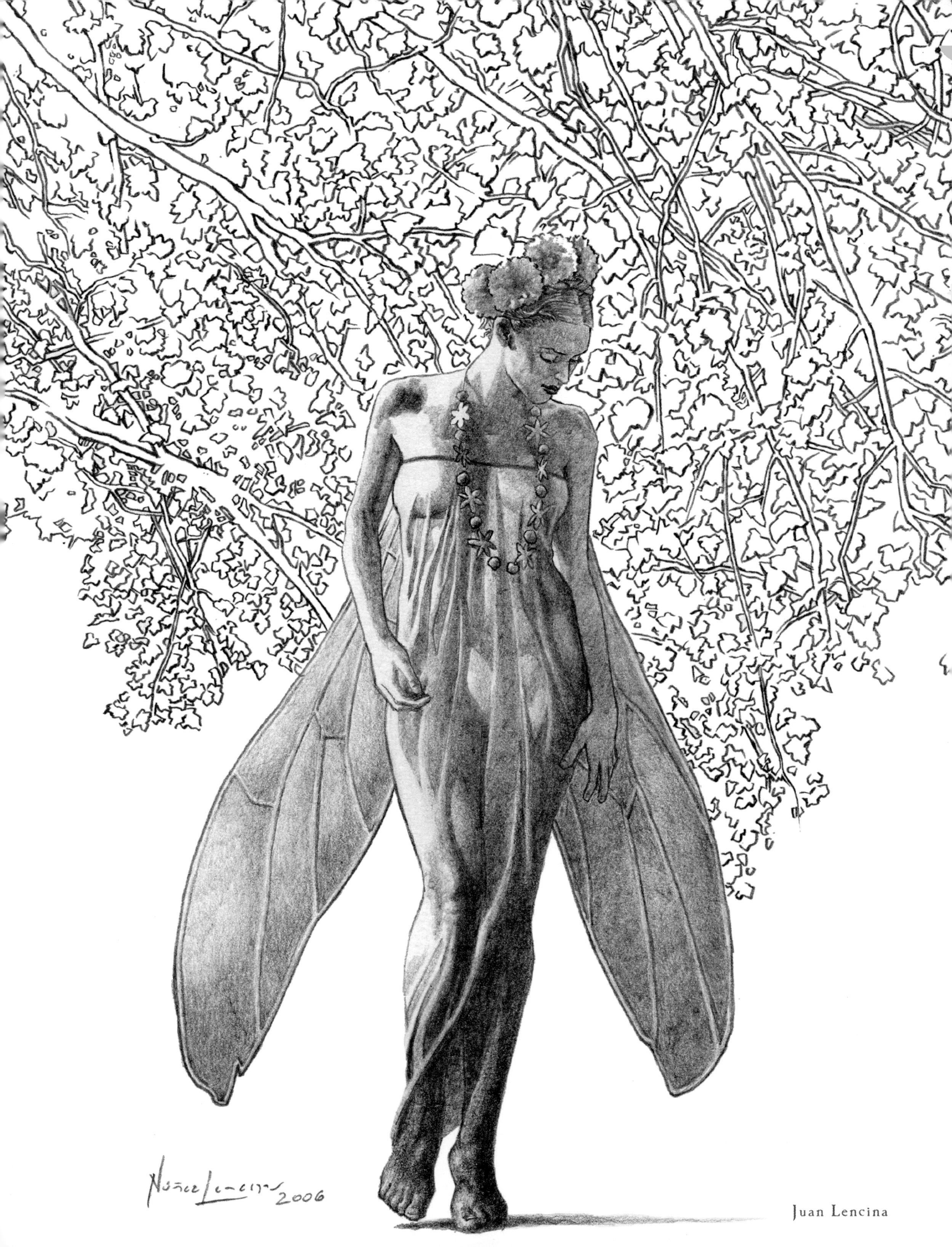

Juan Lencina

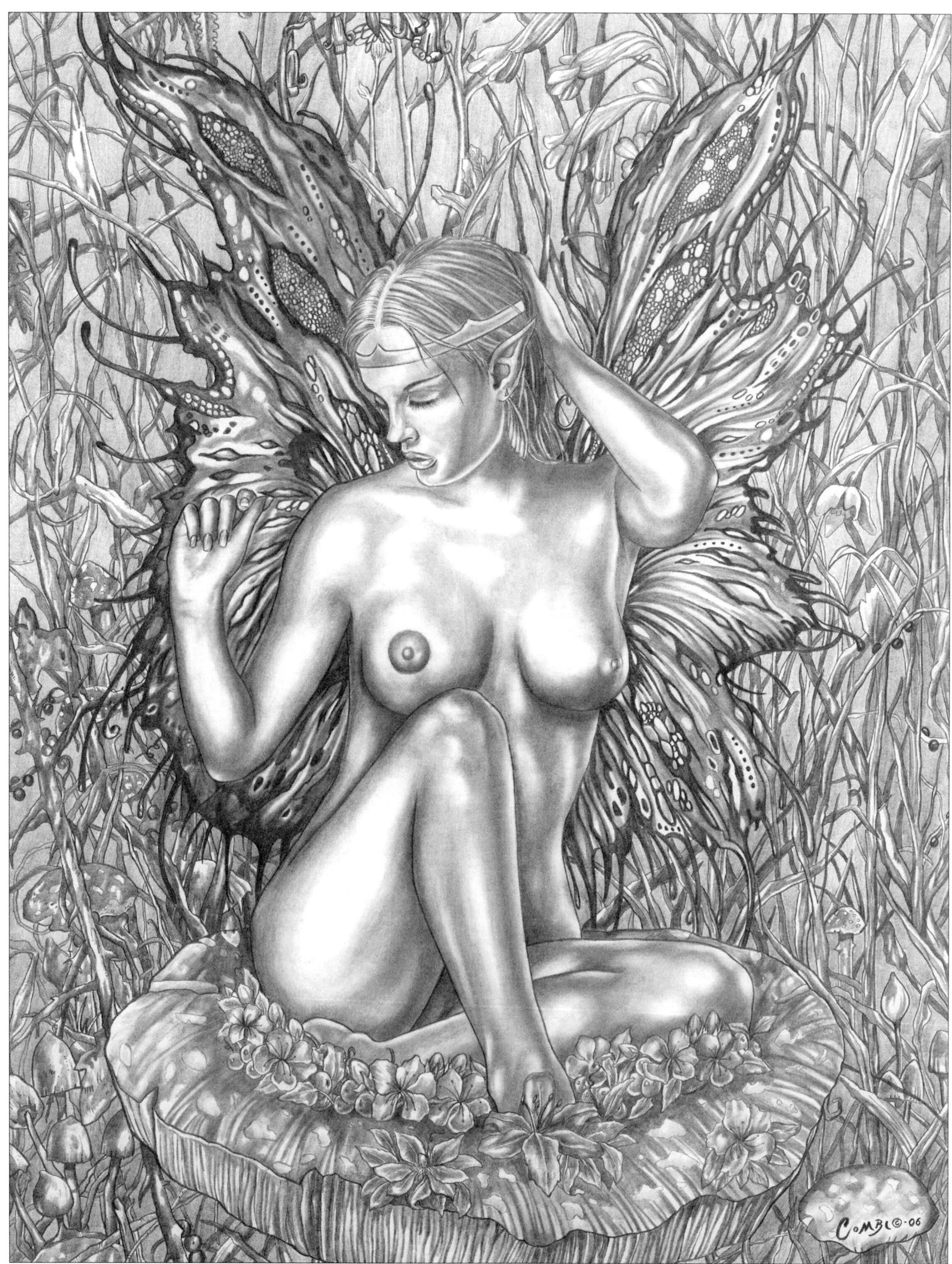

Federico Combi

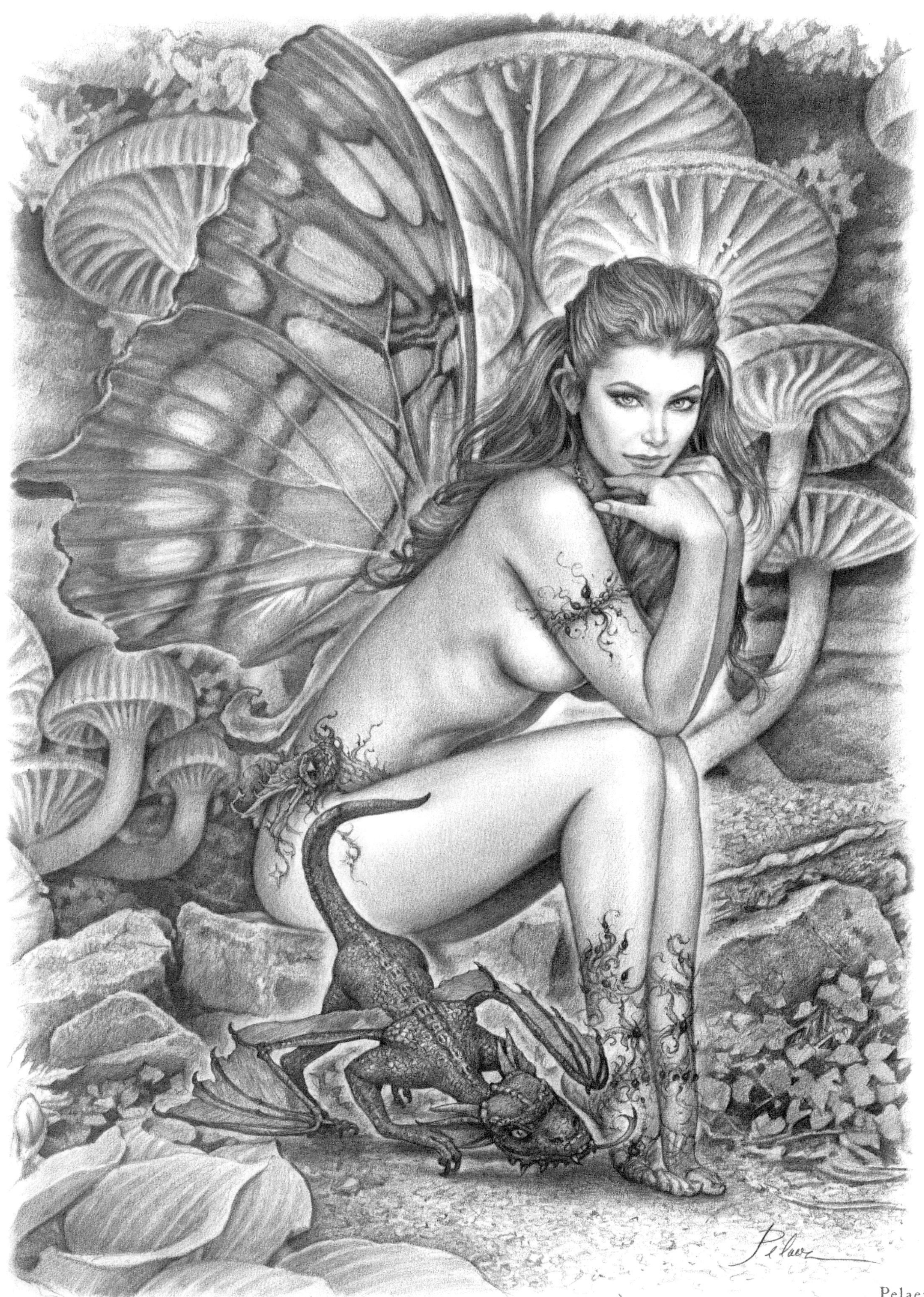

Pelaez

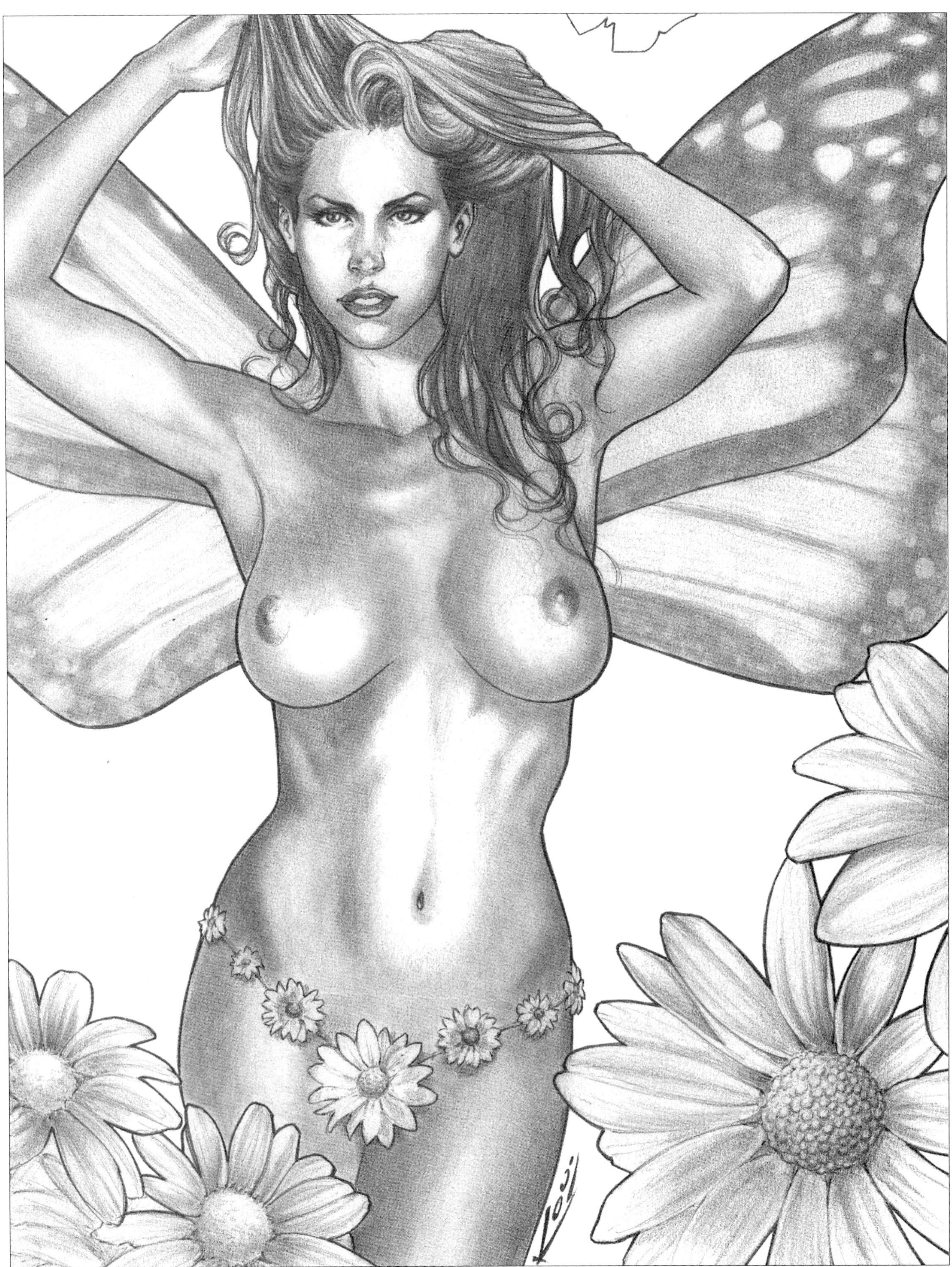

Pablo Kousovitis

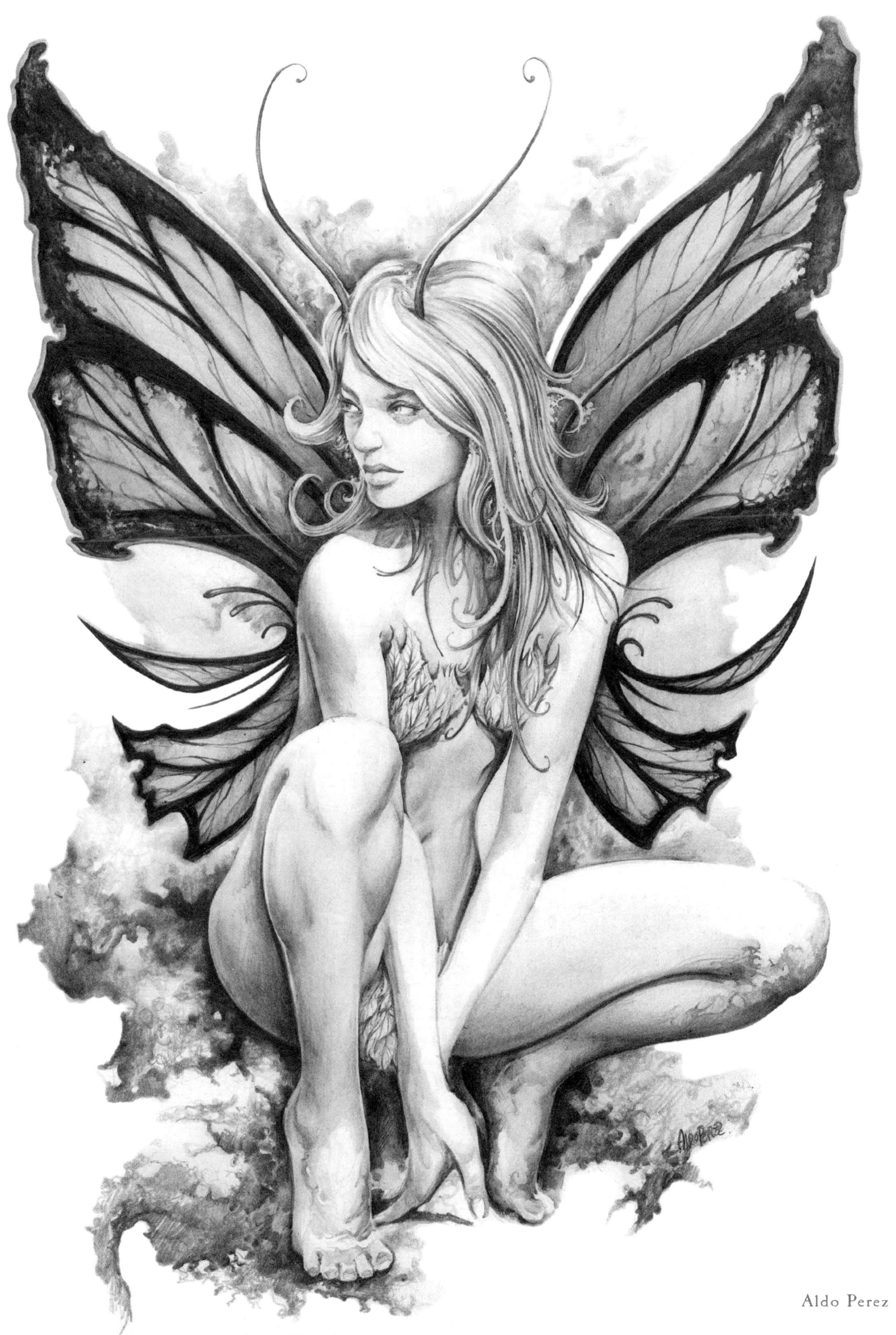

Aldo Perez

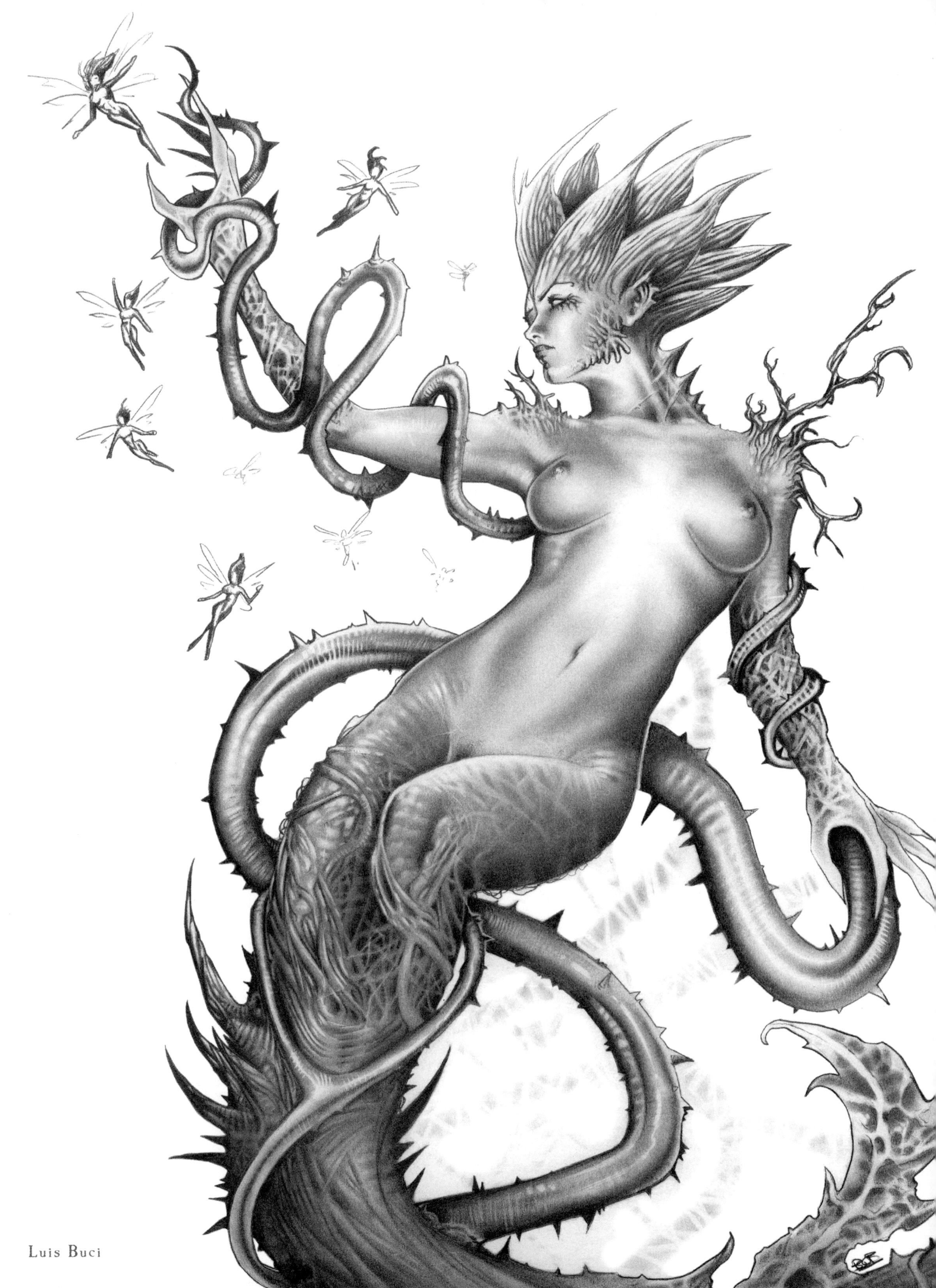

Luis Buci

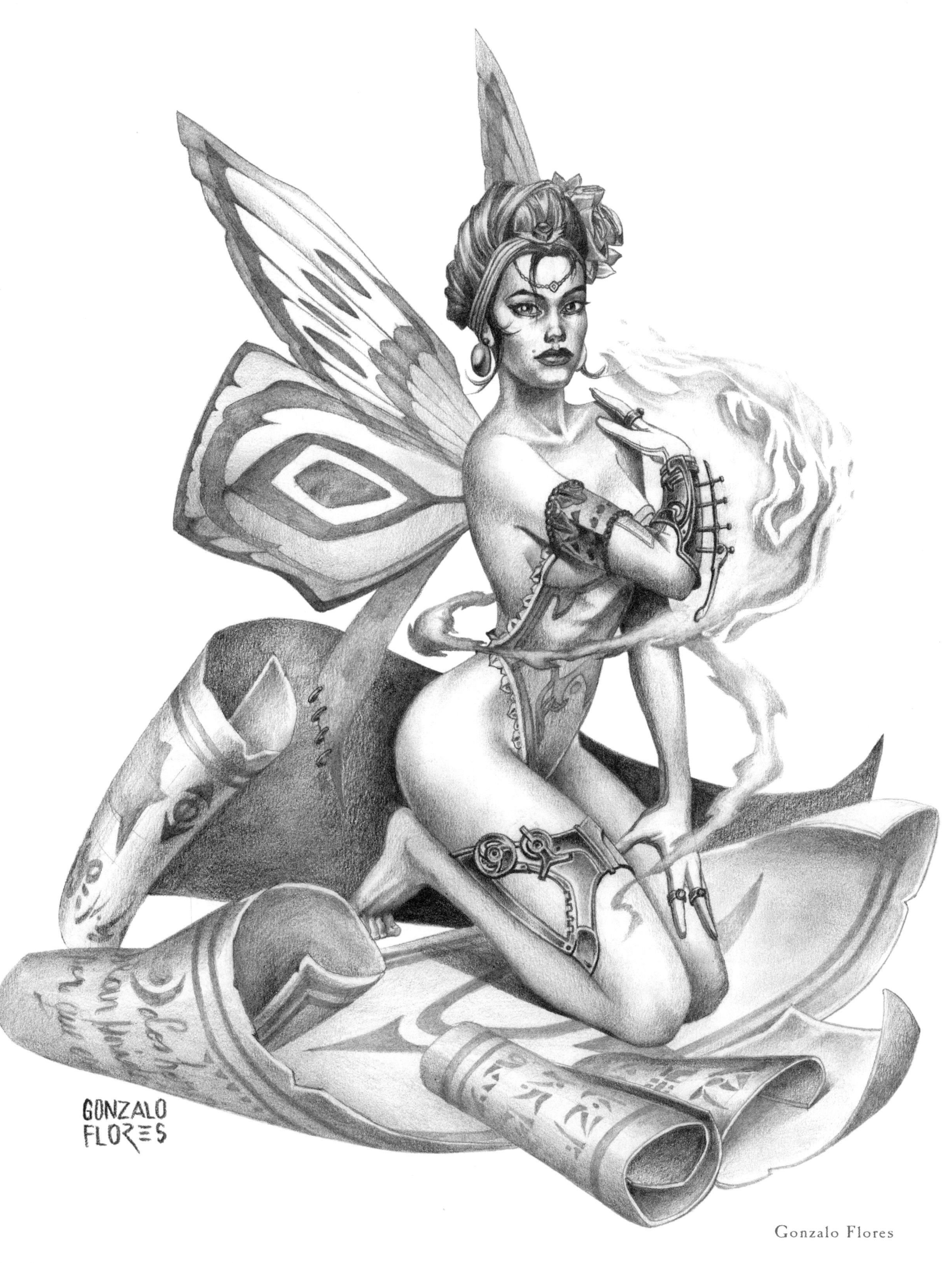

Gonzalo Flores

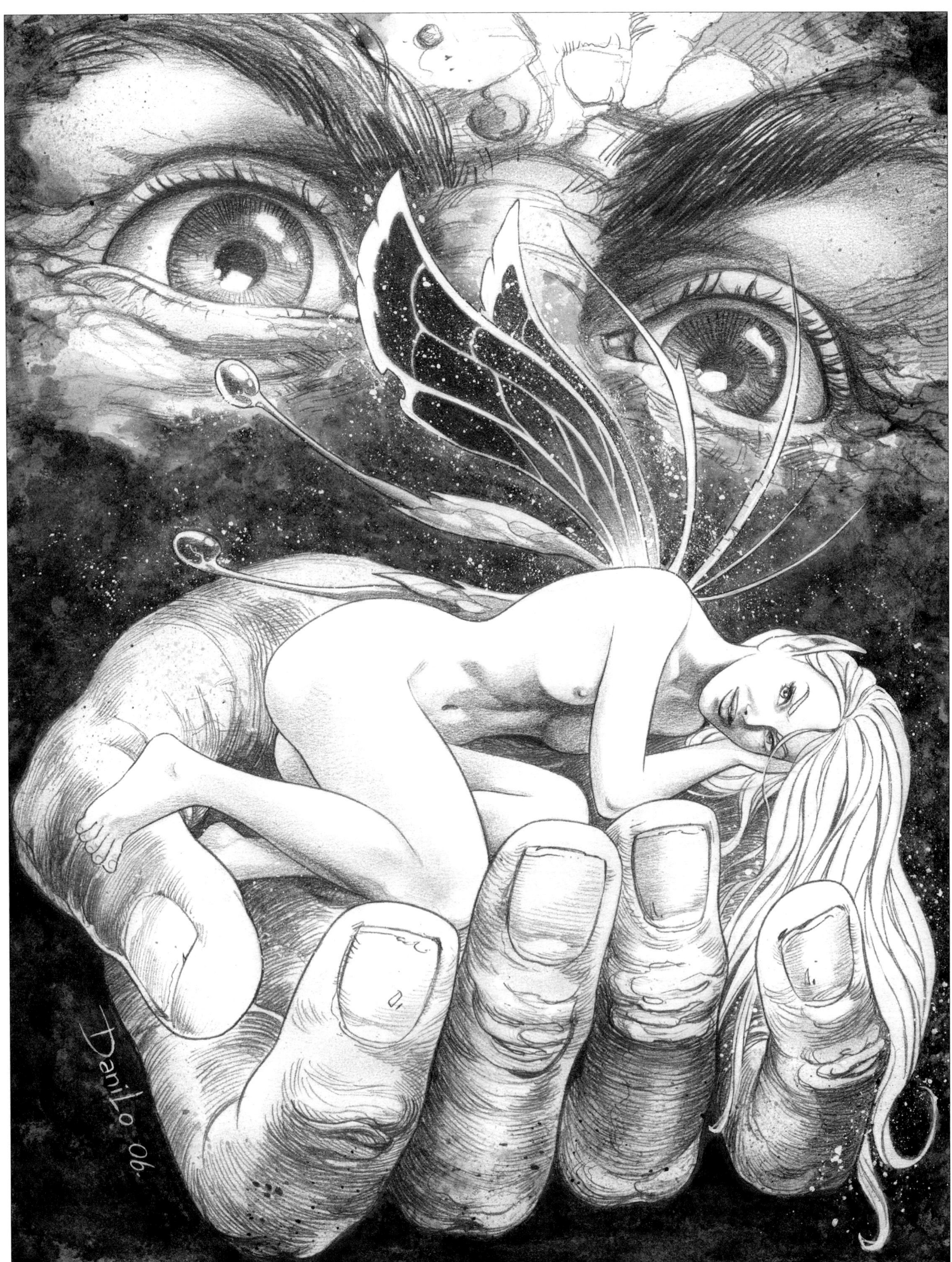

Danilo Guida

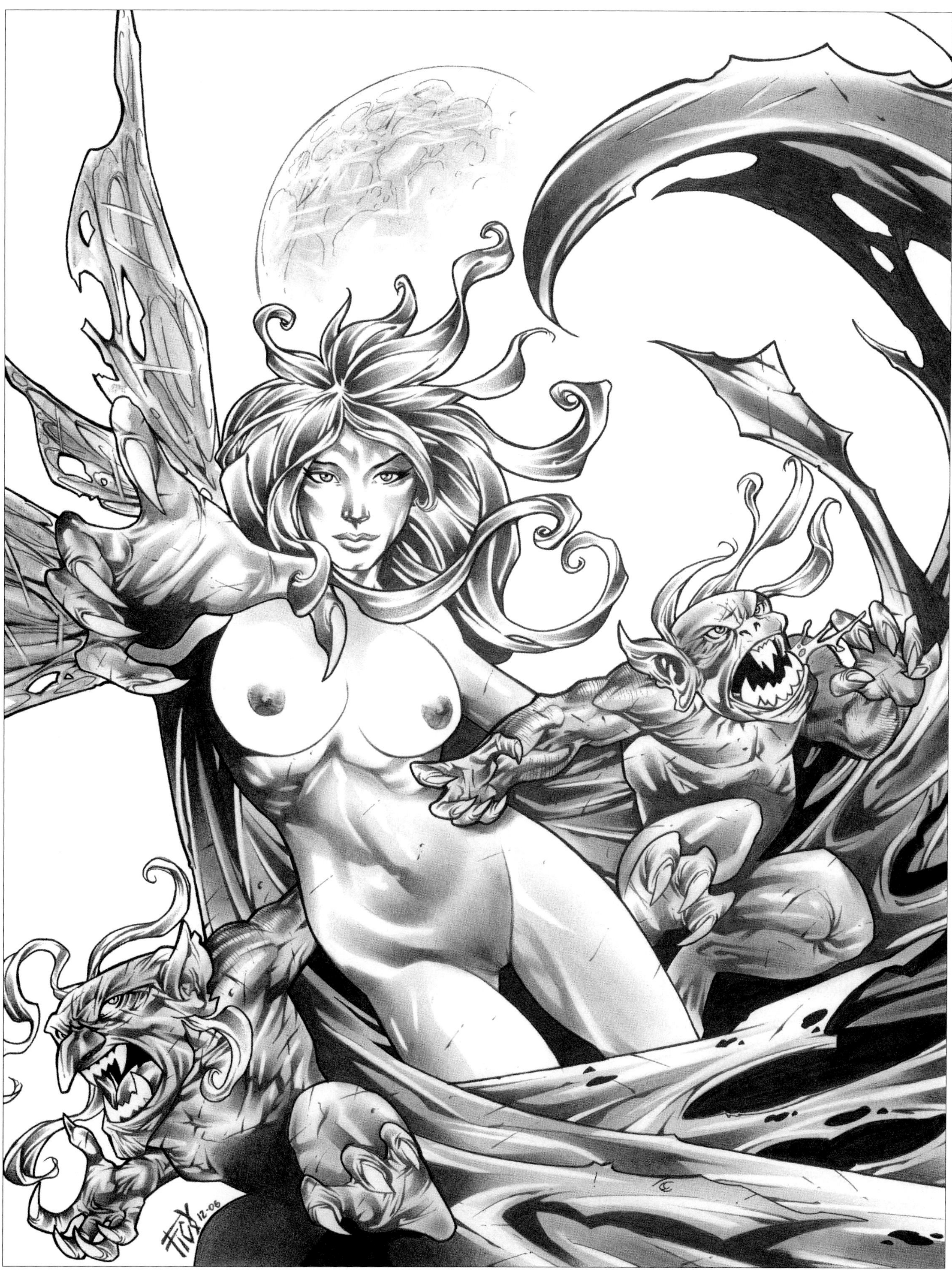

Federico Ossio

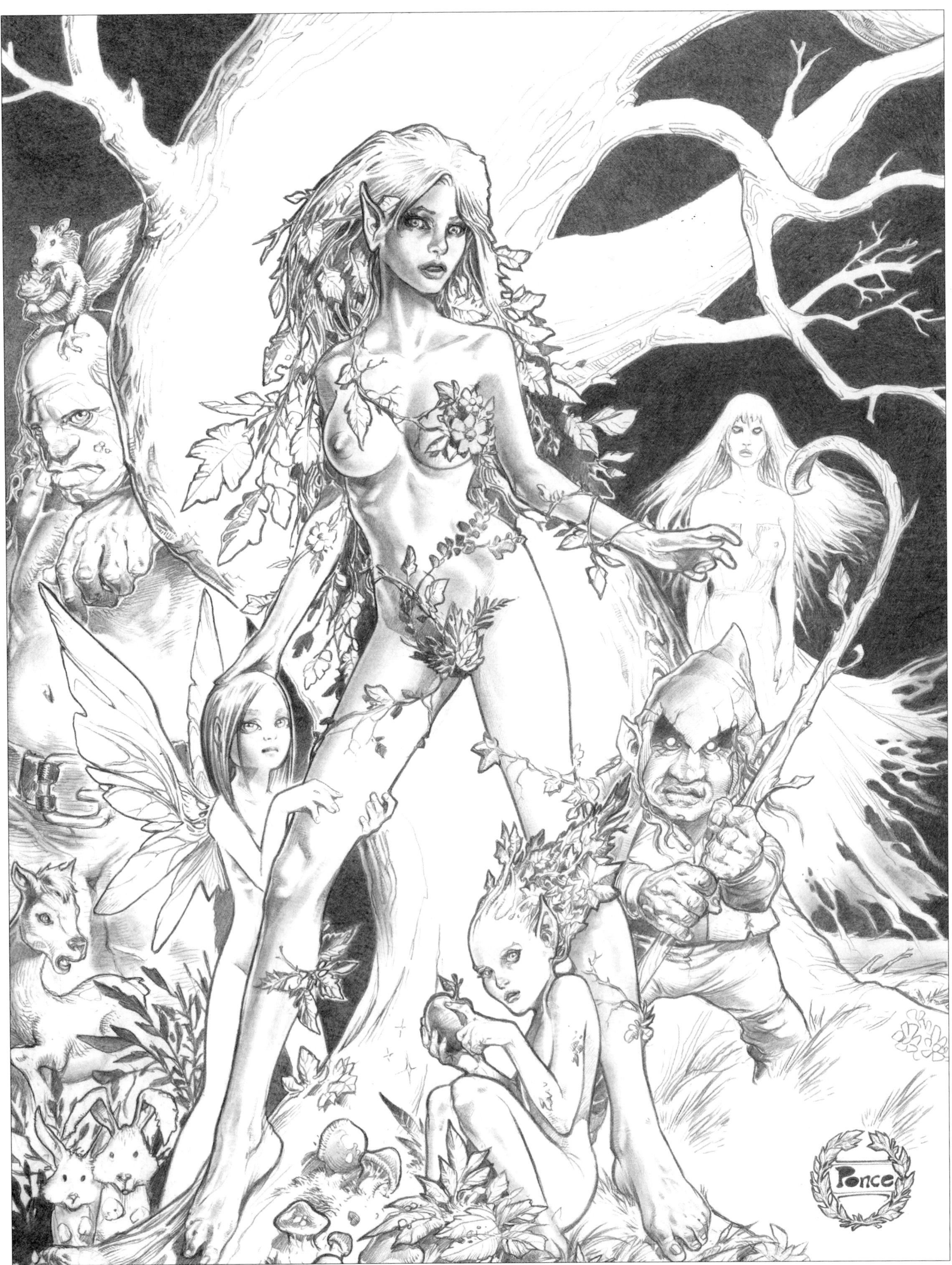

German Ponce

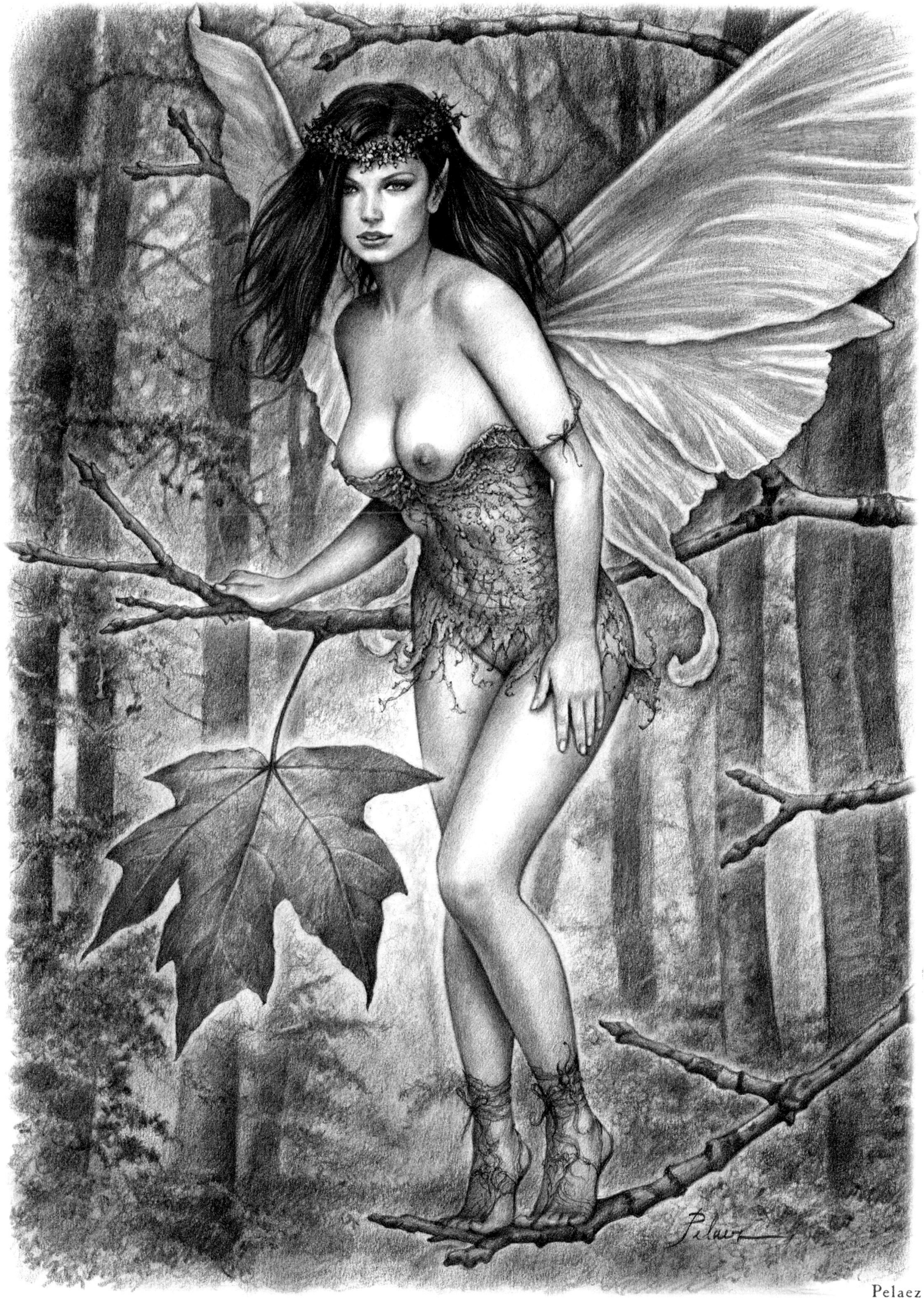

Pelaez

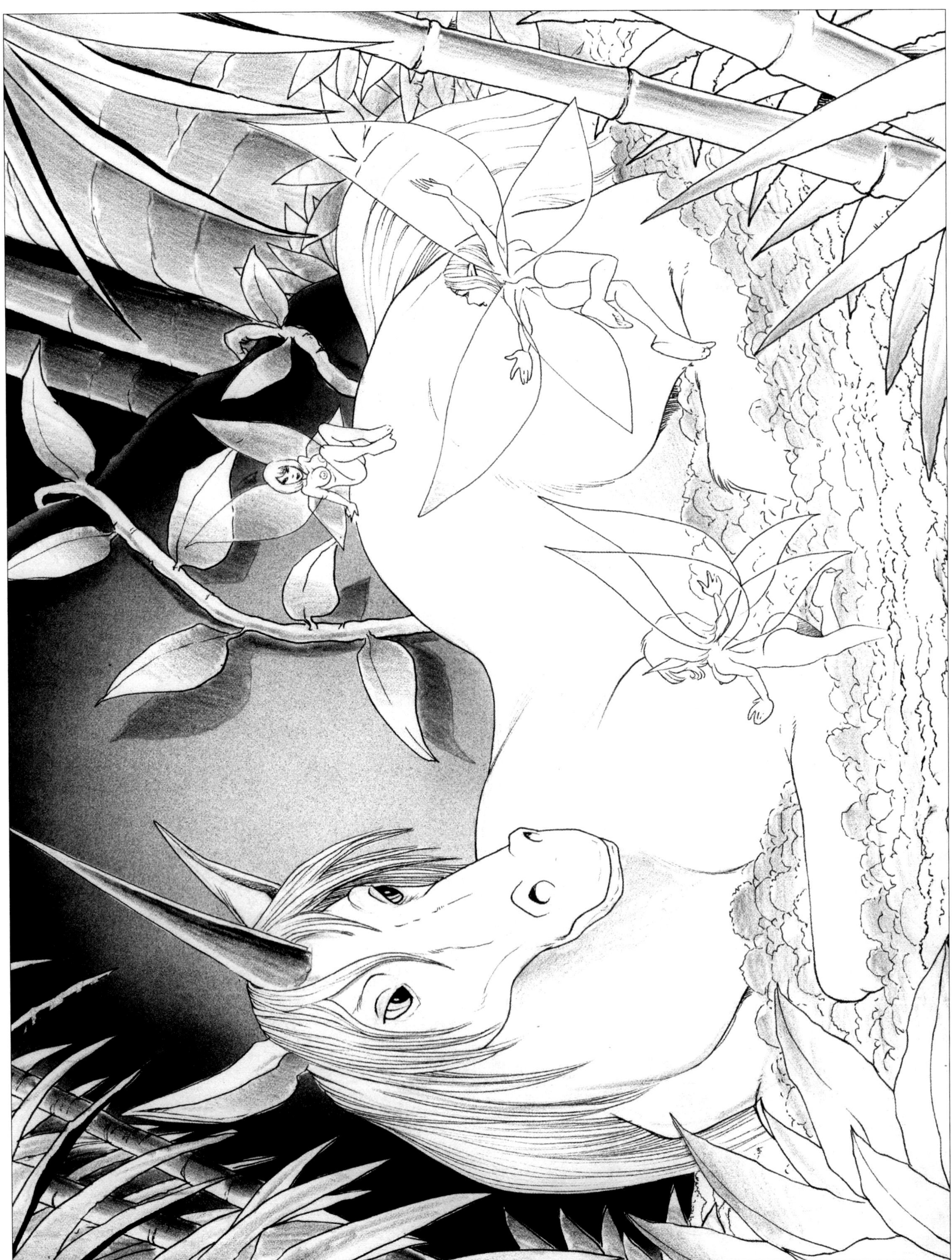

Barry Blair

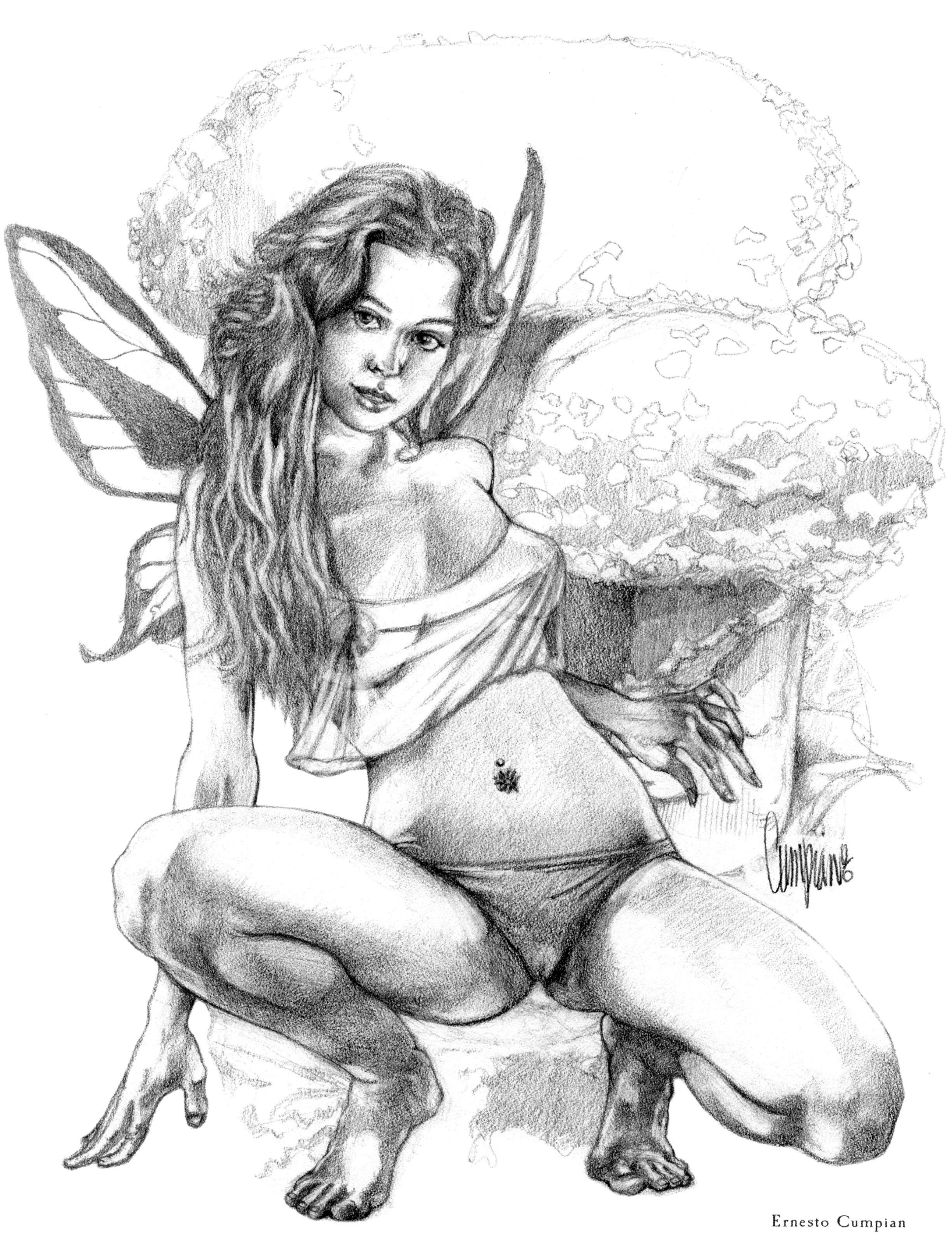

Ernesto Cumpian

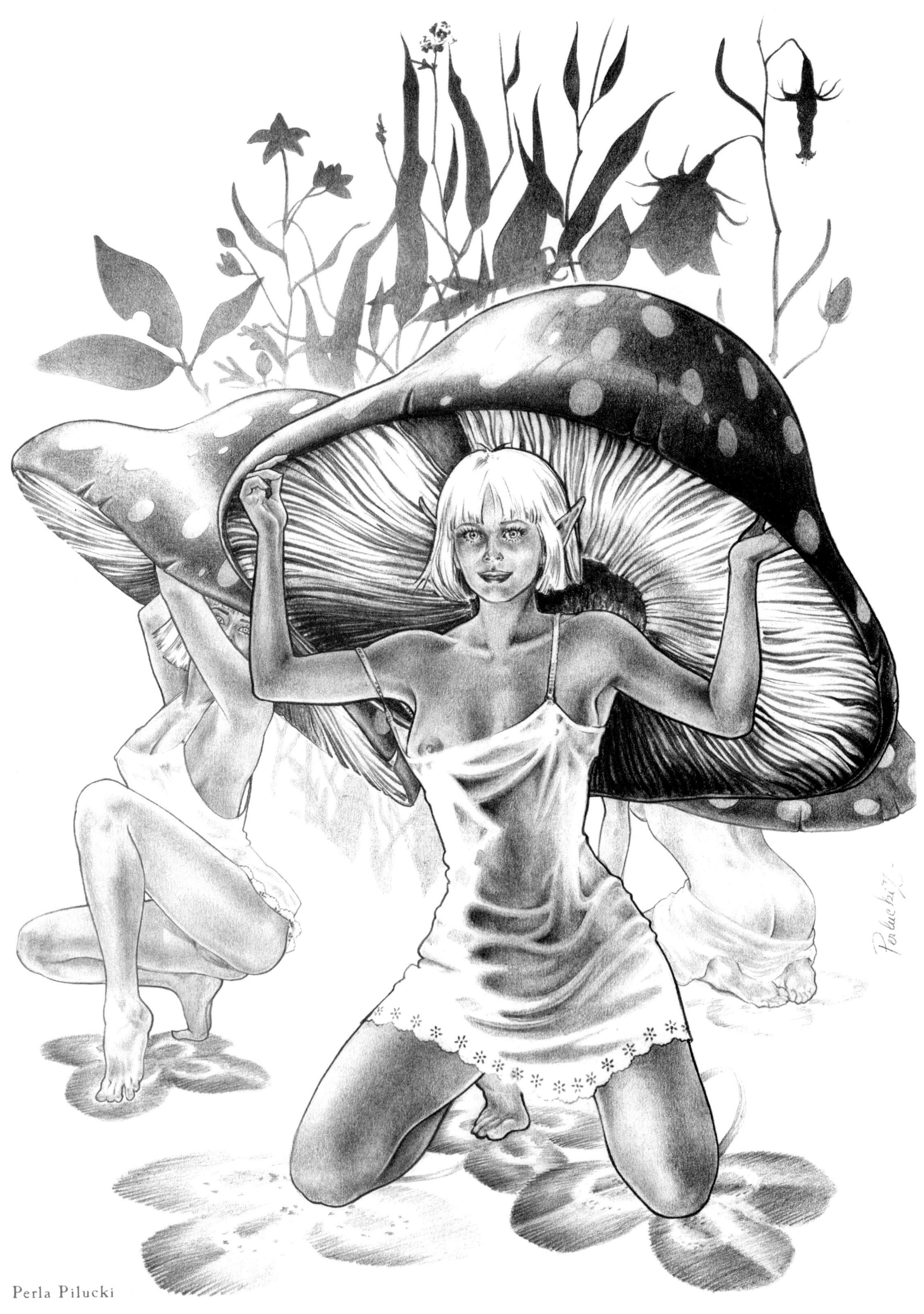

Perla Pilucki

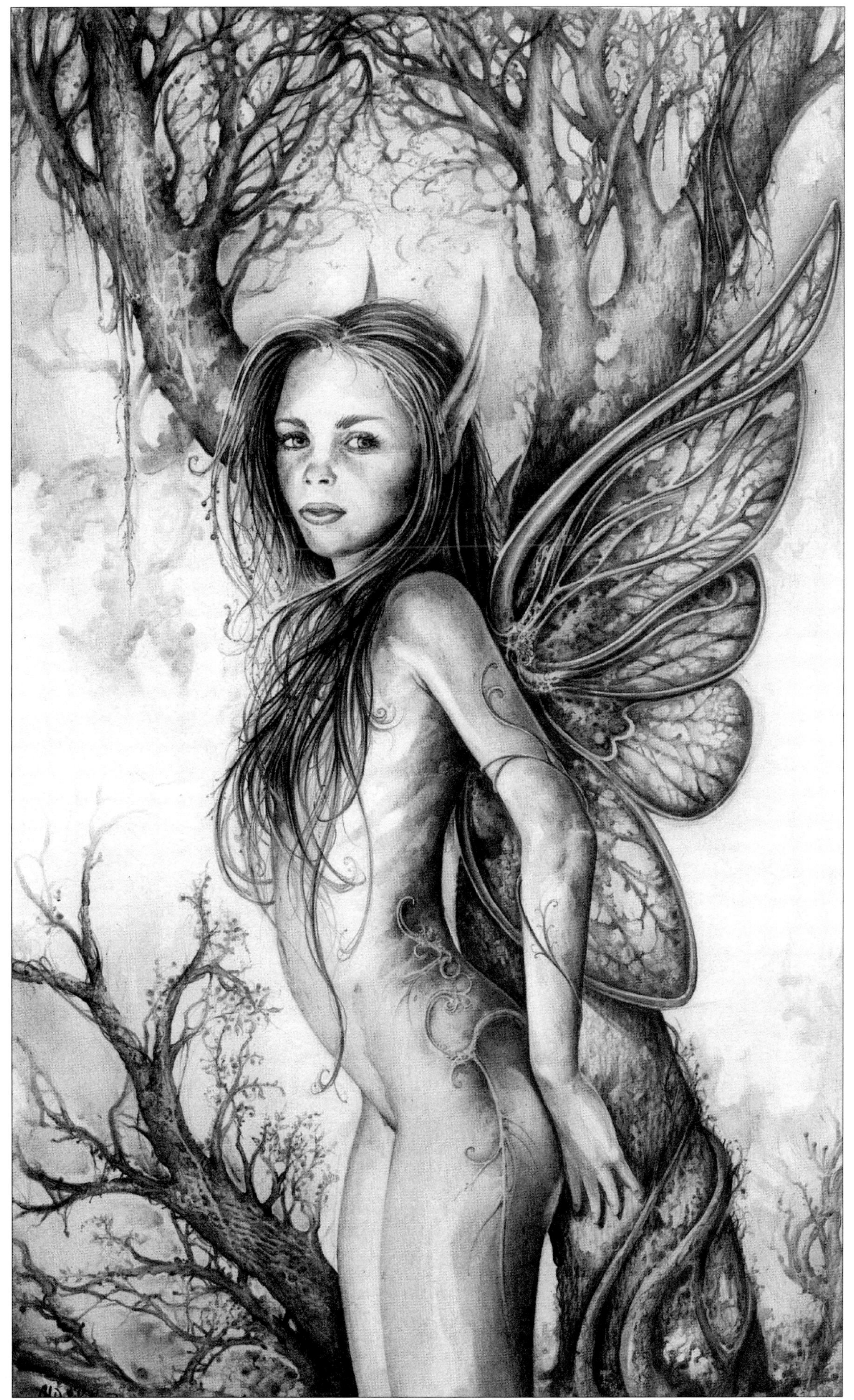

Aldo Perez

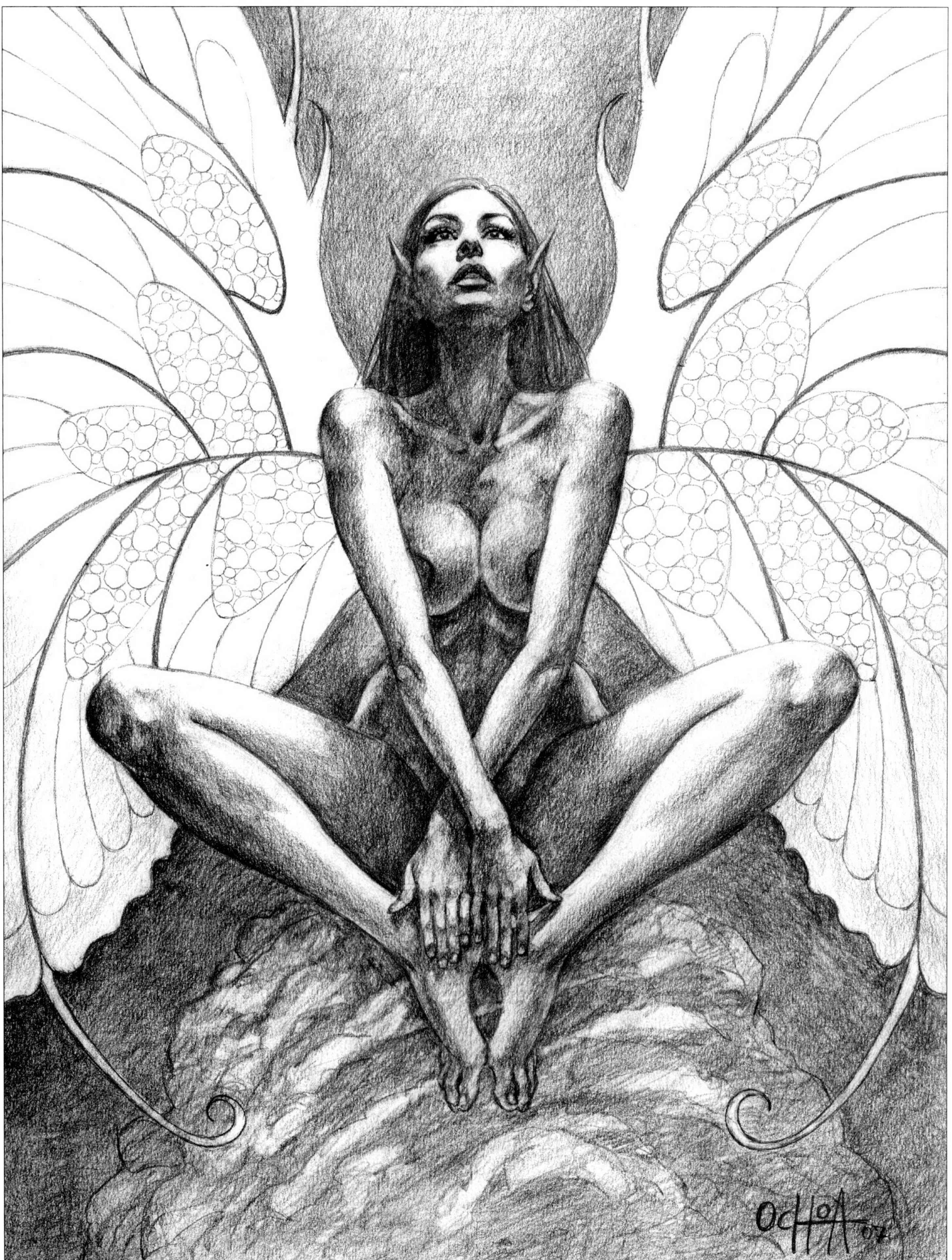

Percy Ochoa

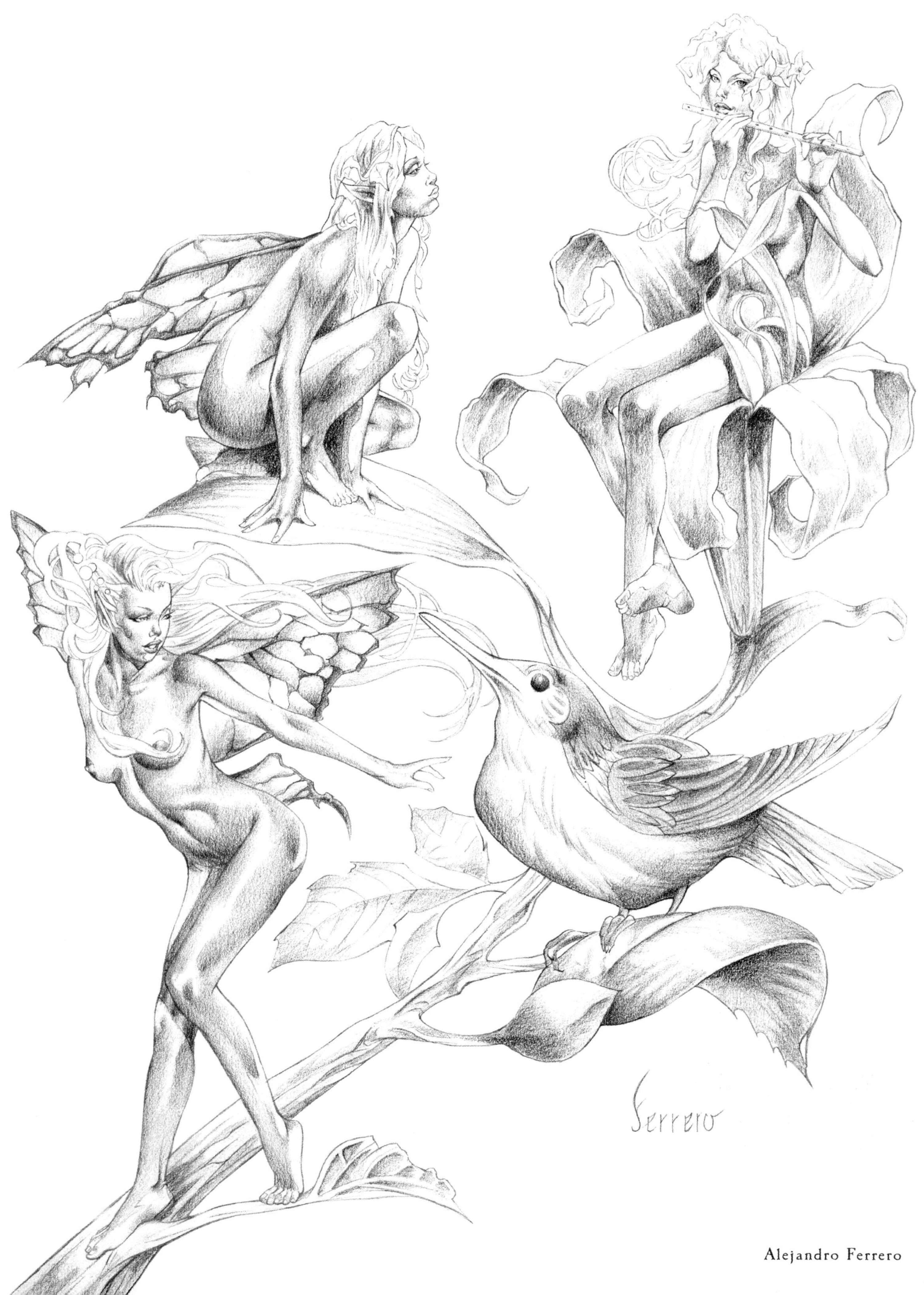

Alejandro Ferrero

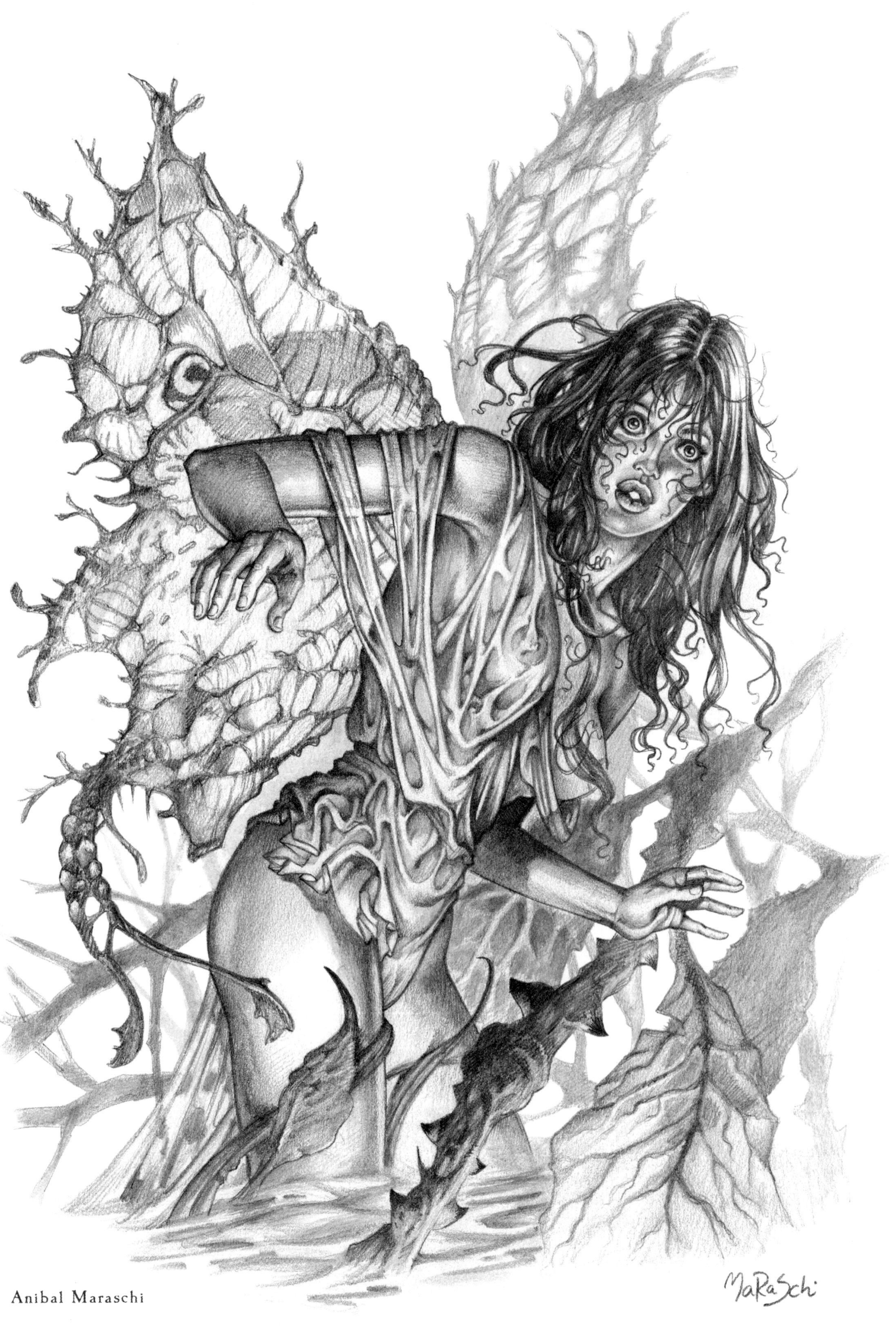

Anibal Maraschi

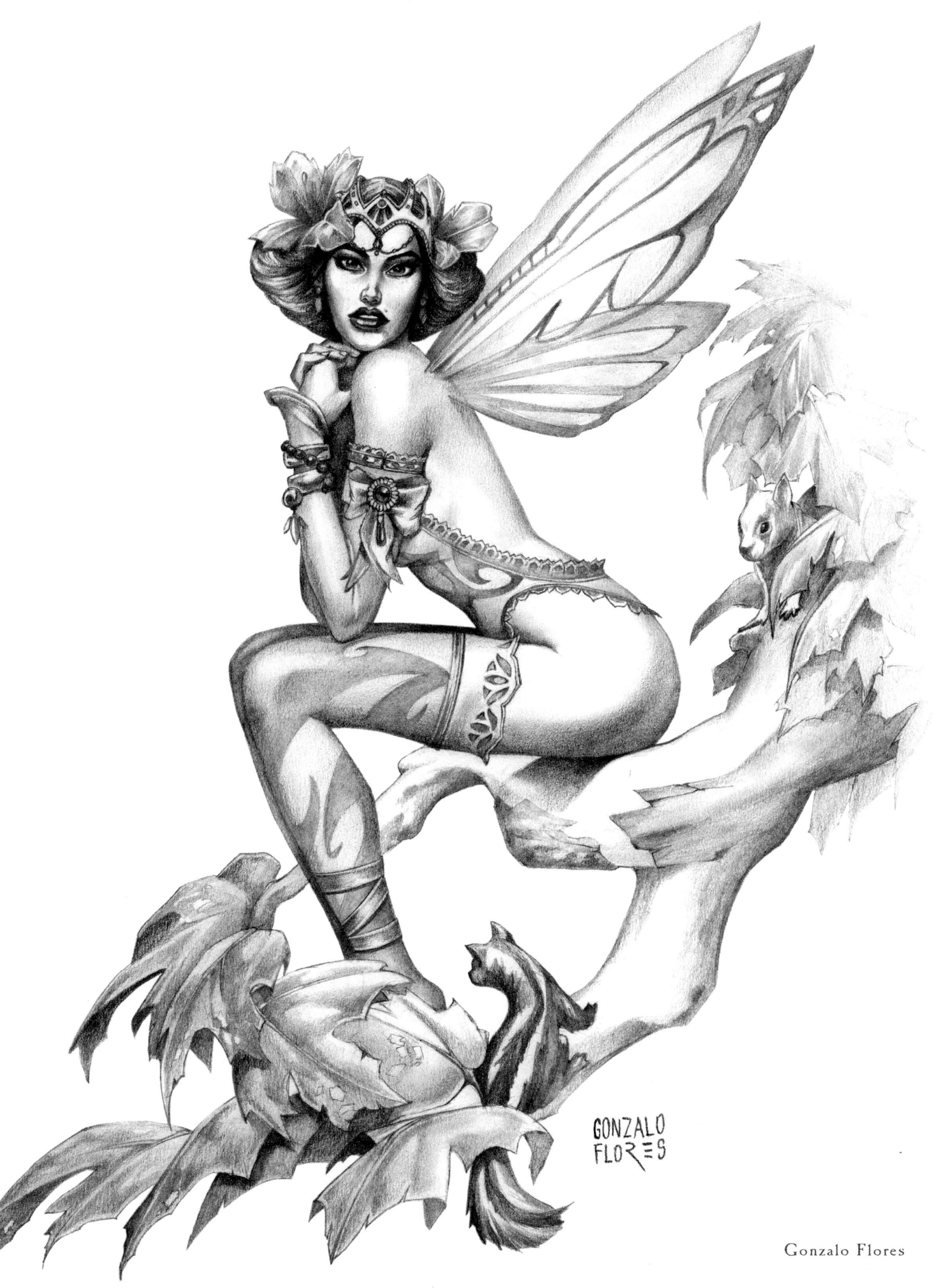

Gonzalo Flores

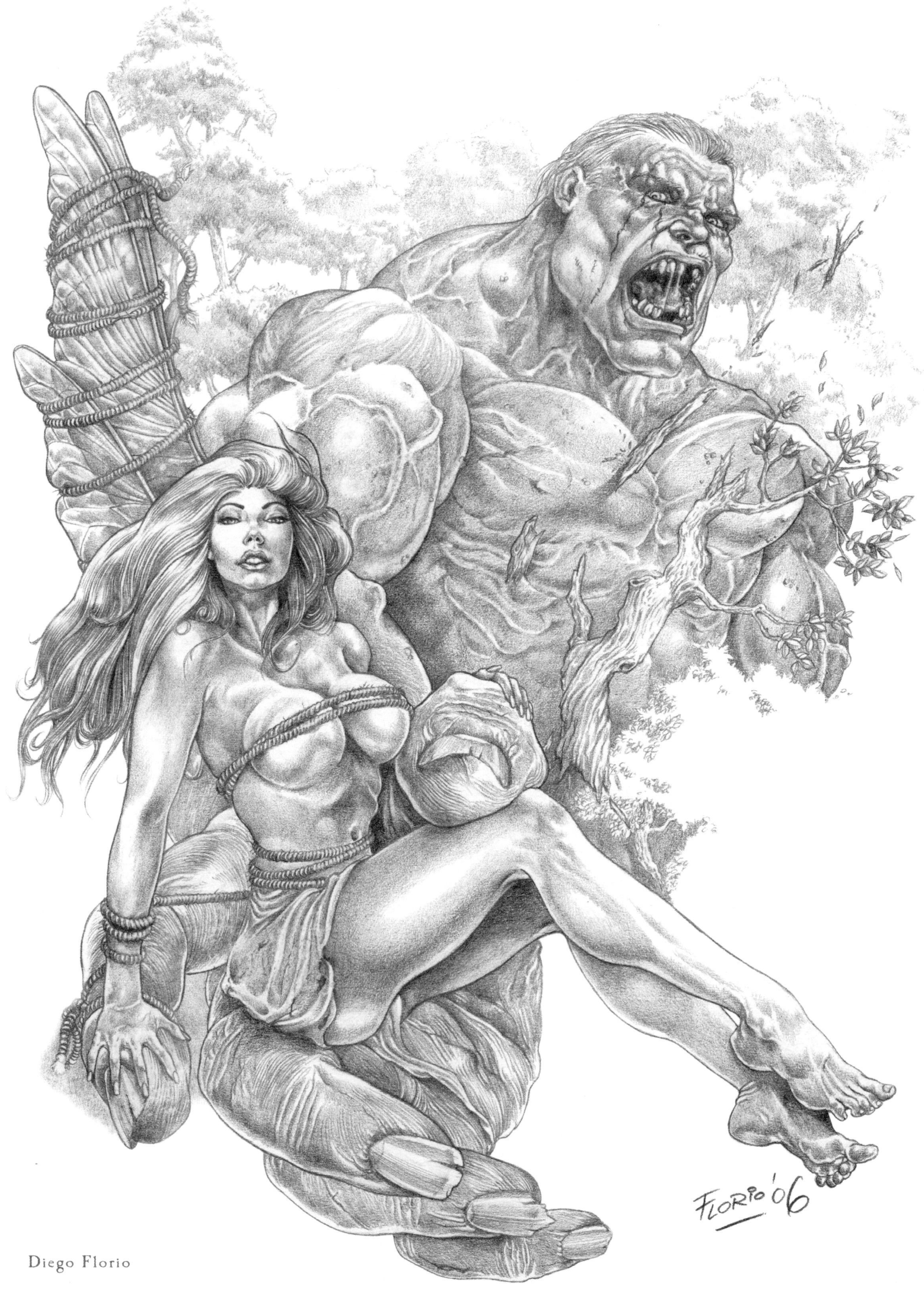

Diego Florio

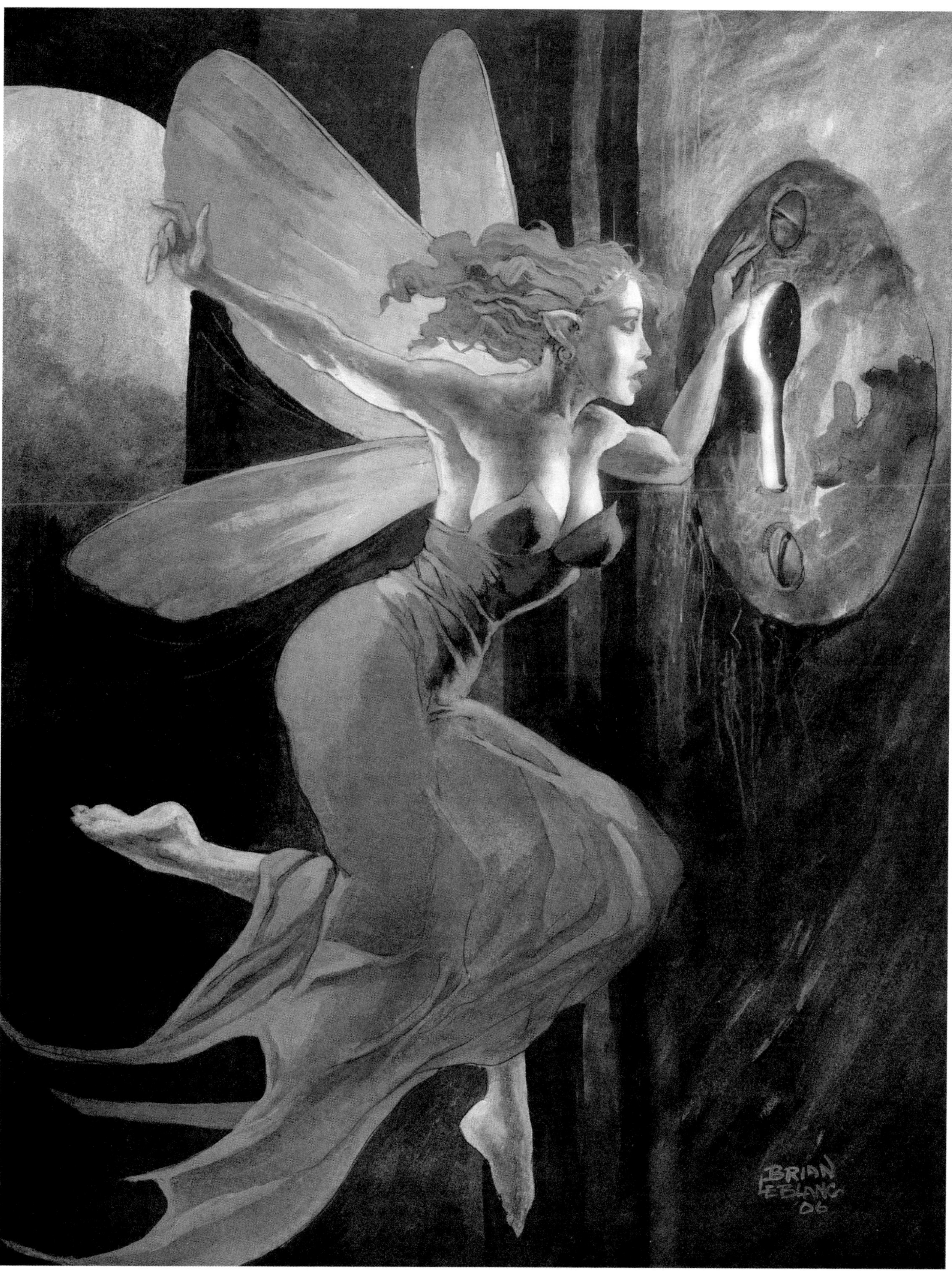

Brian LeBlanc

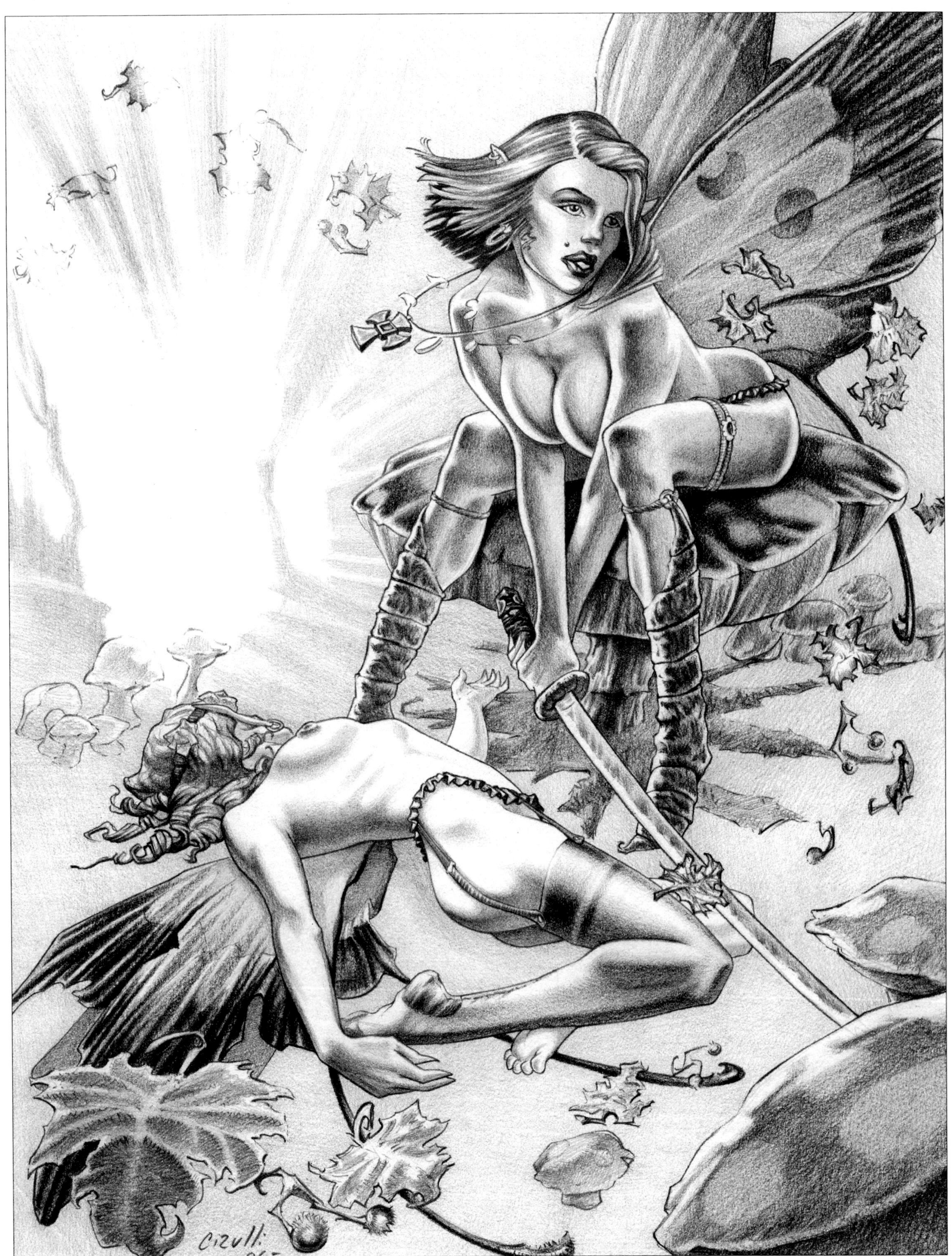

Diego Cirulli

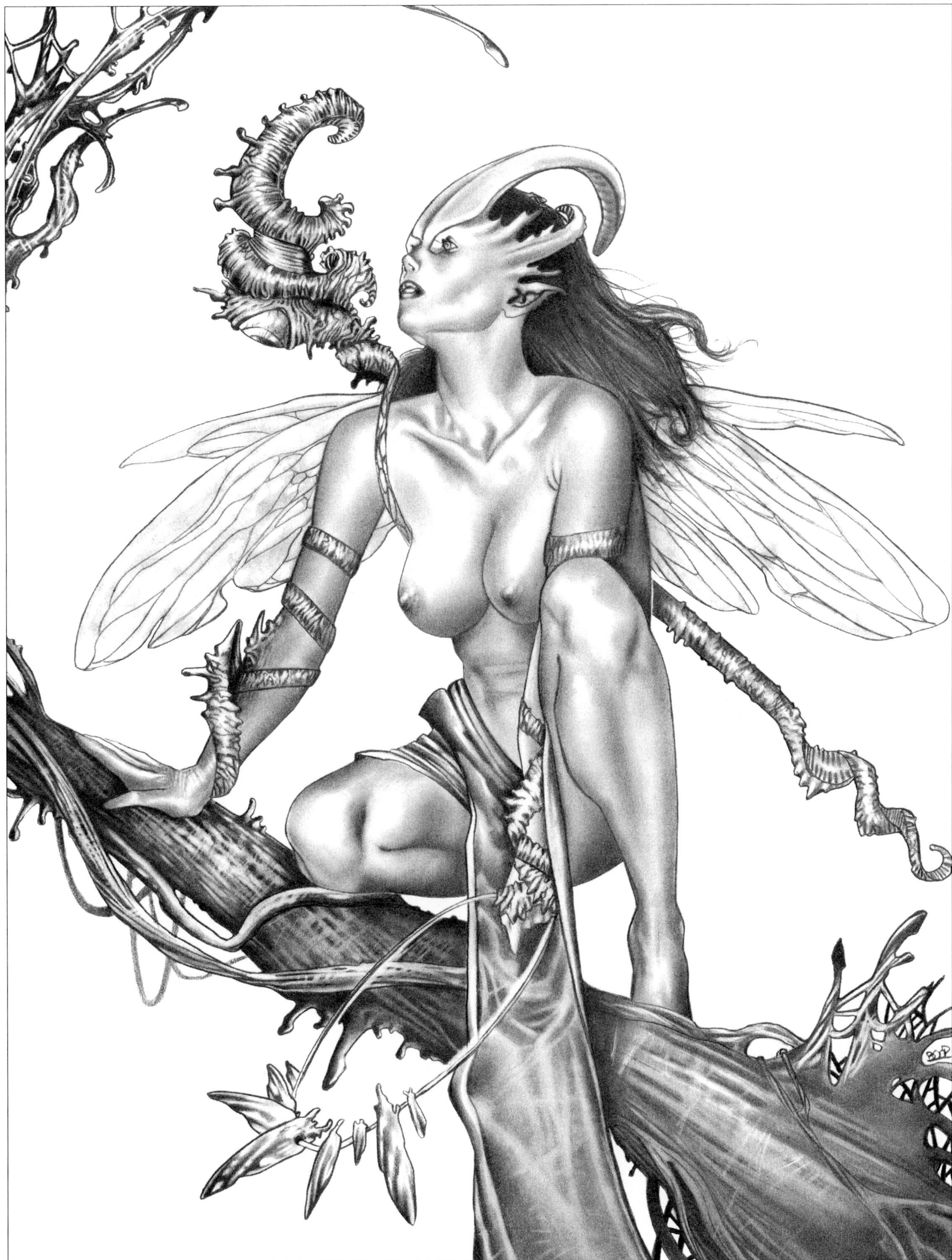

Luis Buci

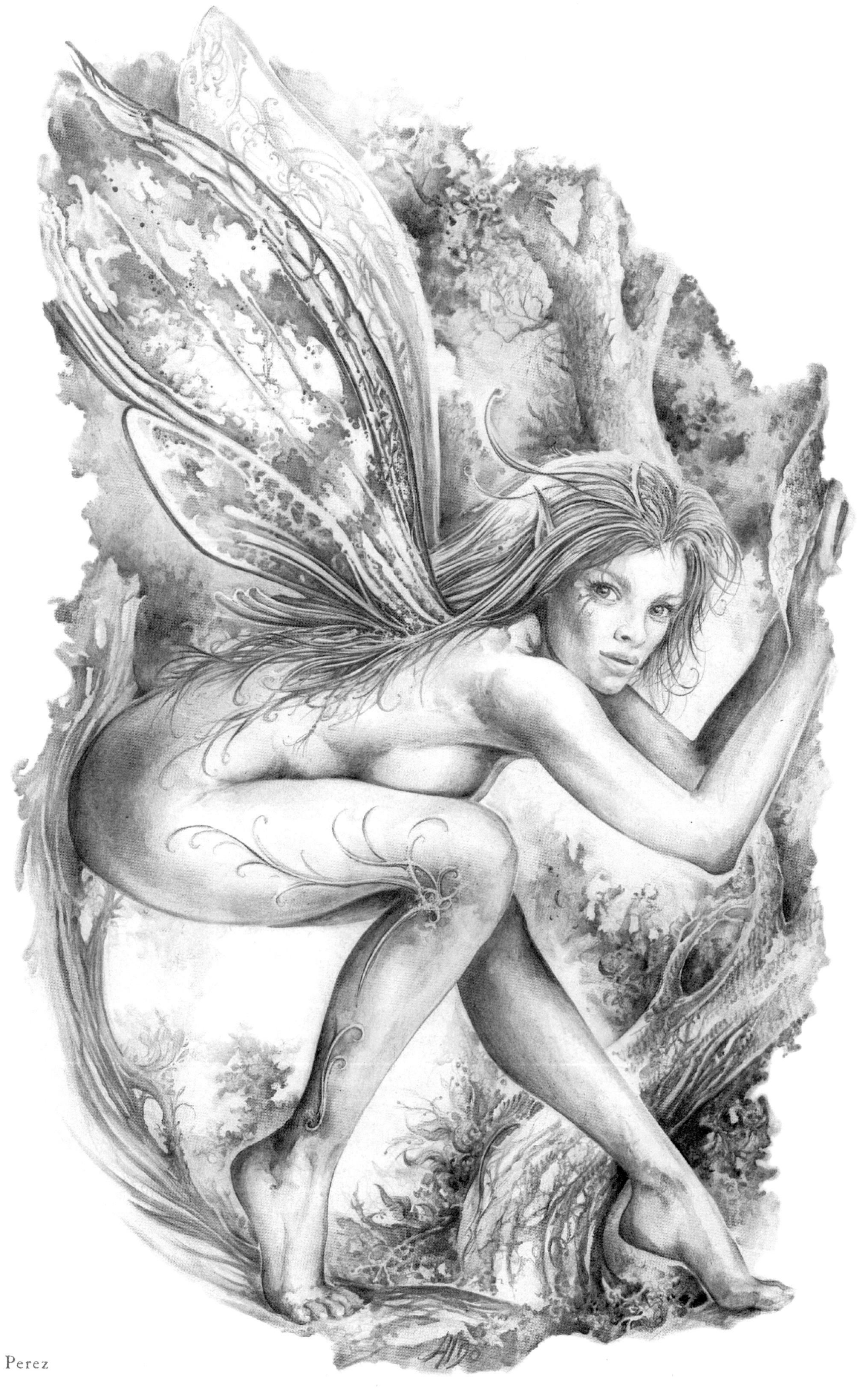

Aldo Perez

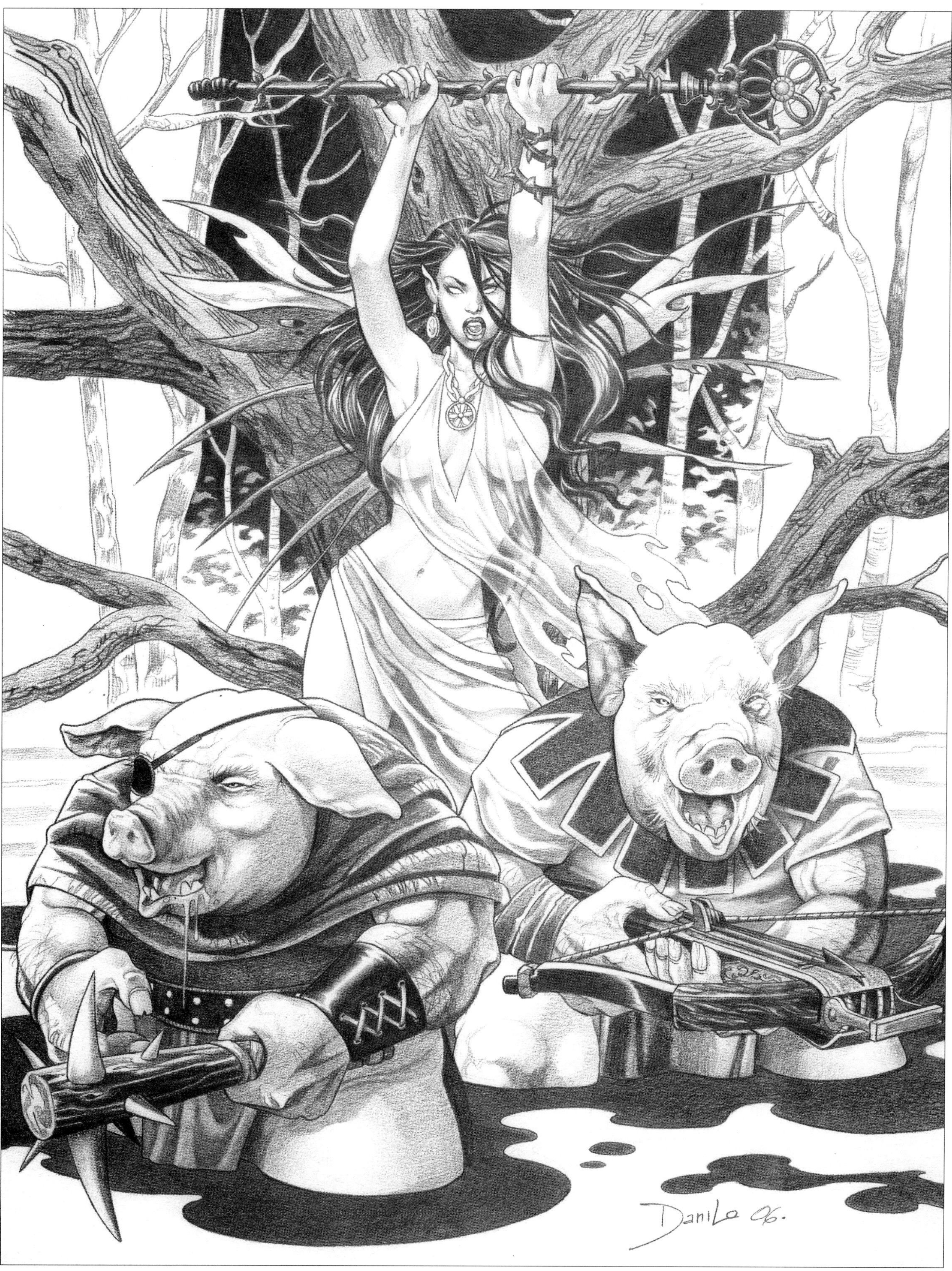

Danilo Guida

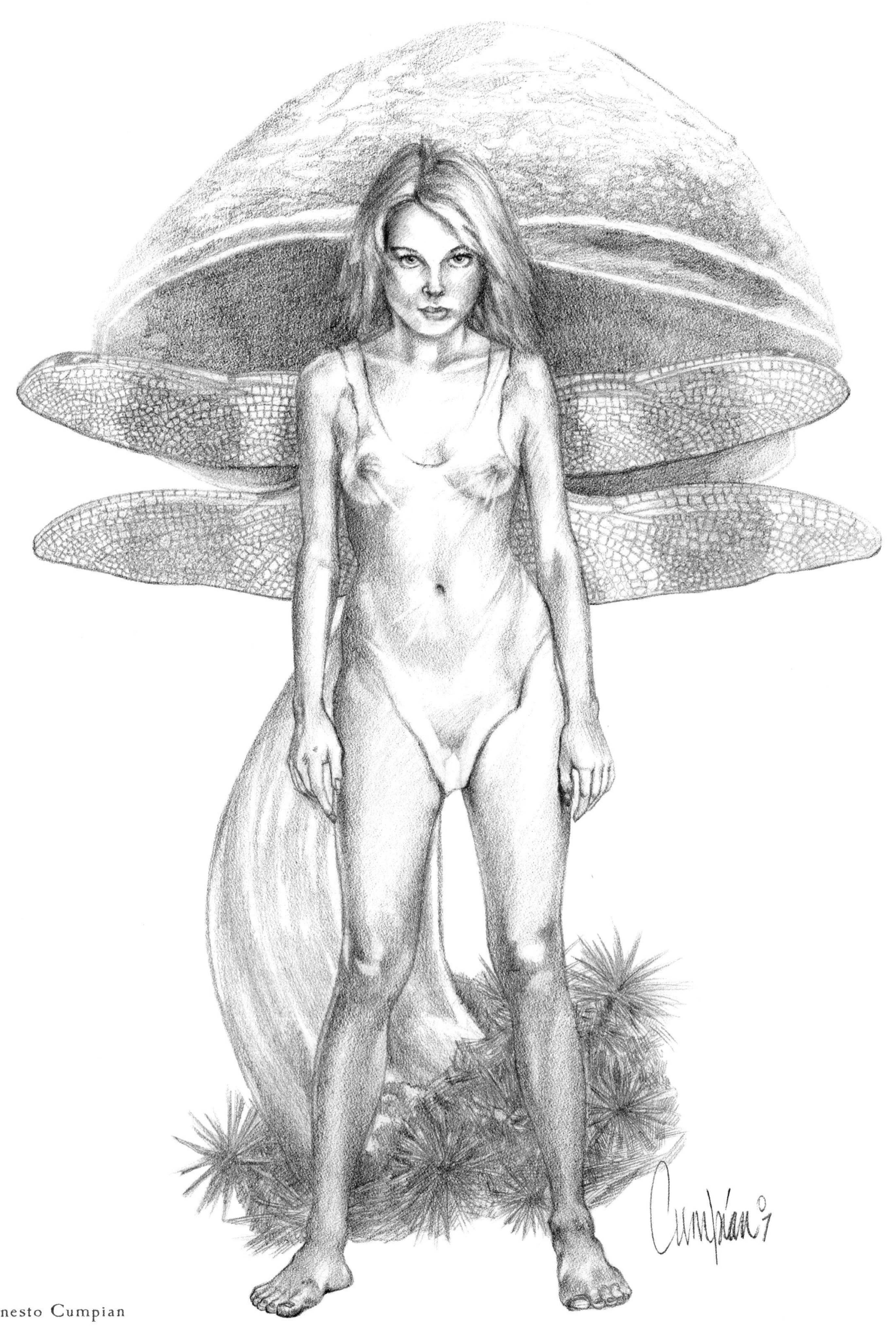

Ernesto Cumpian

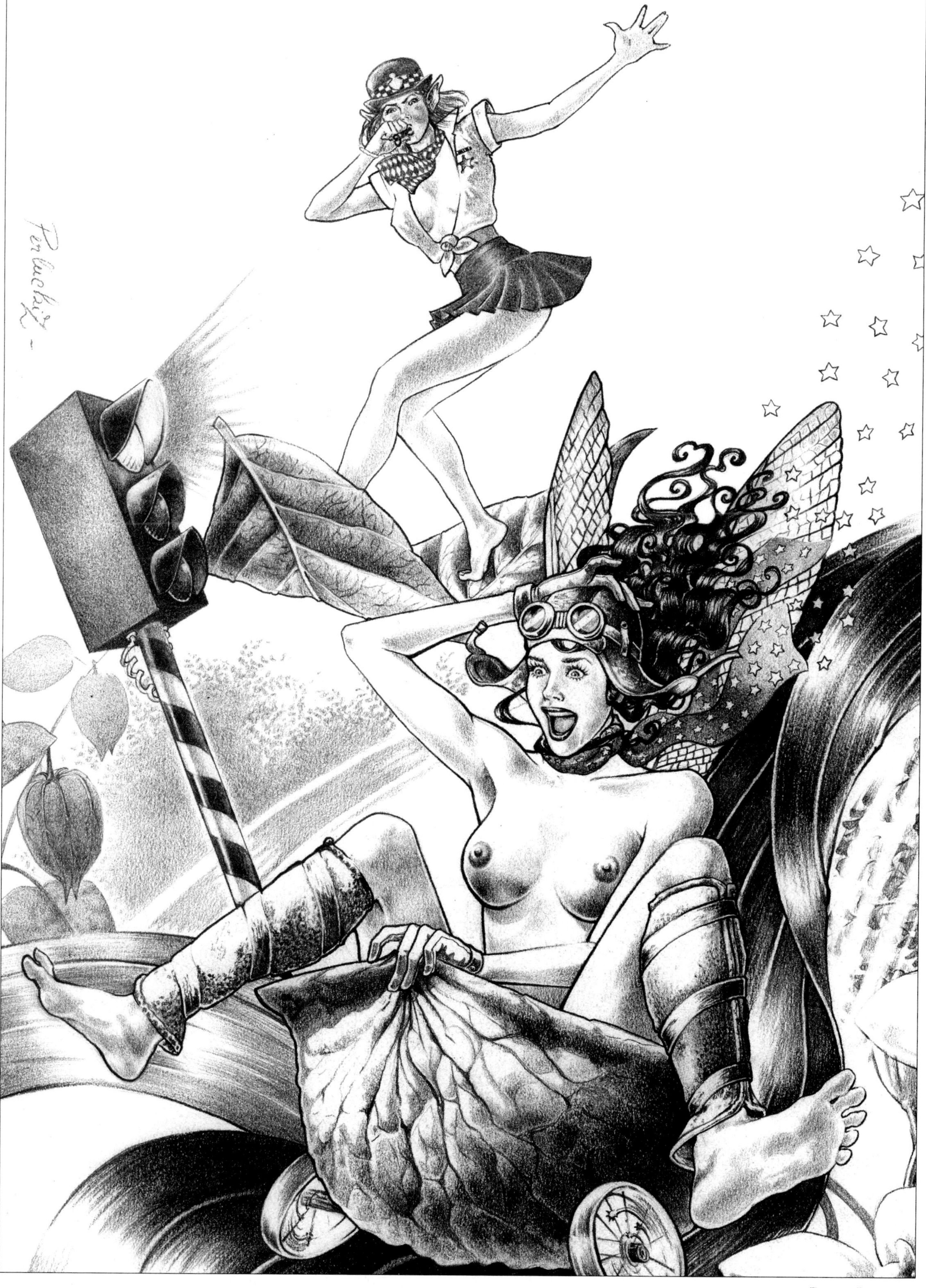

Perla Pilucki

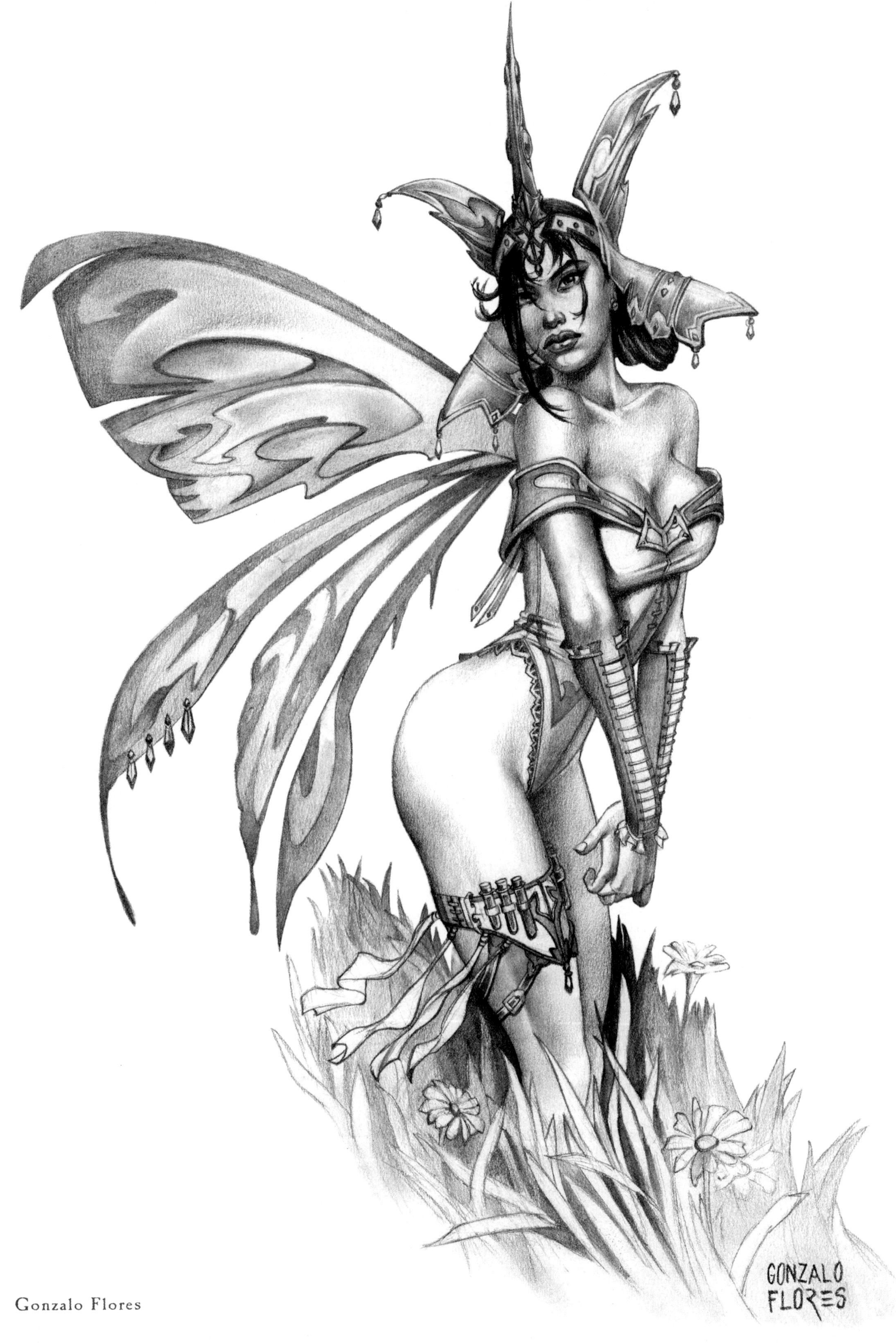

Gonzalo Flores

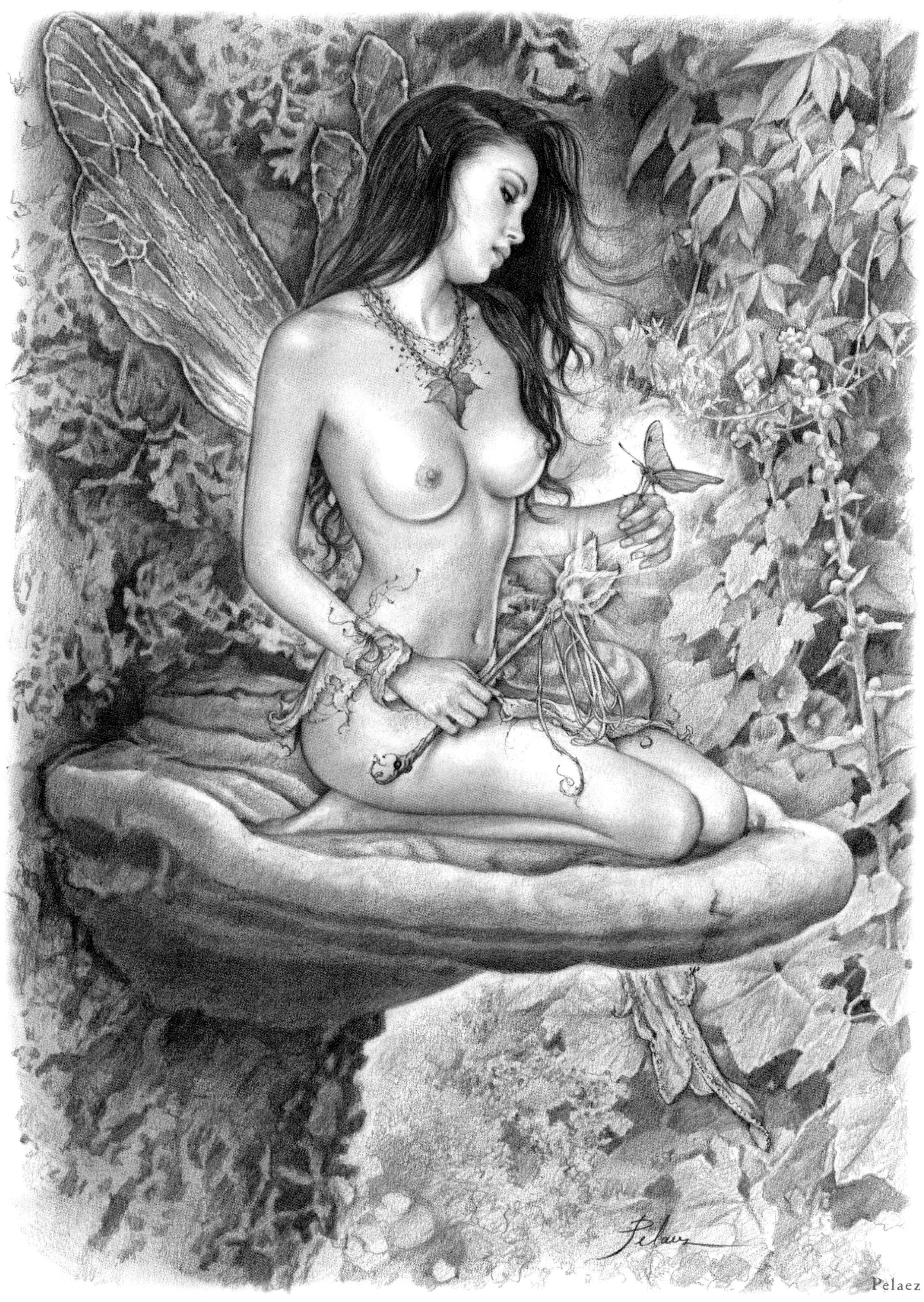

Pelaez

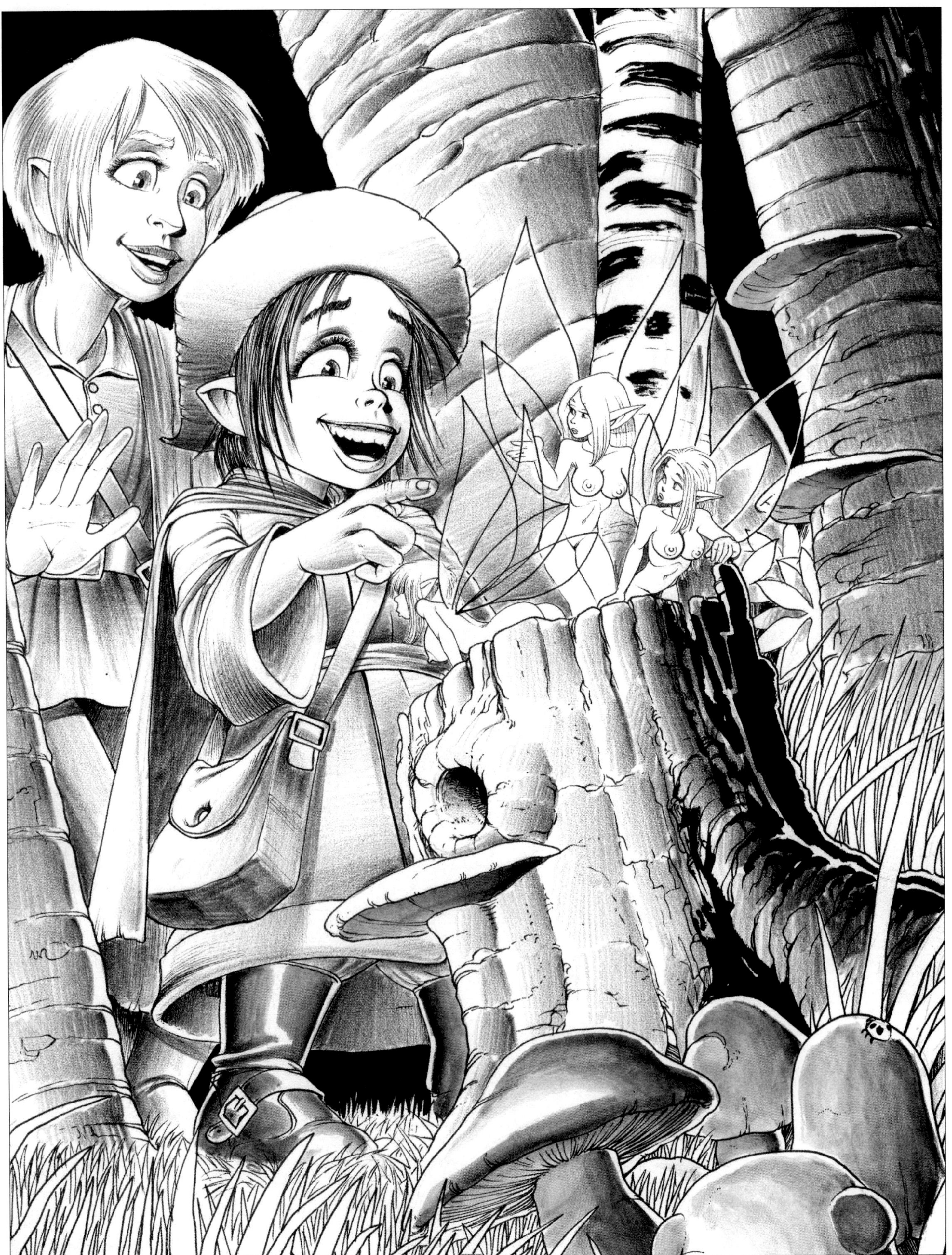

Barry Blair

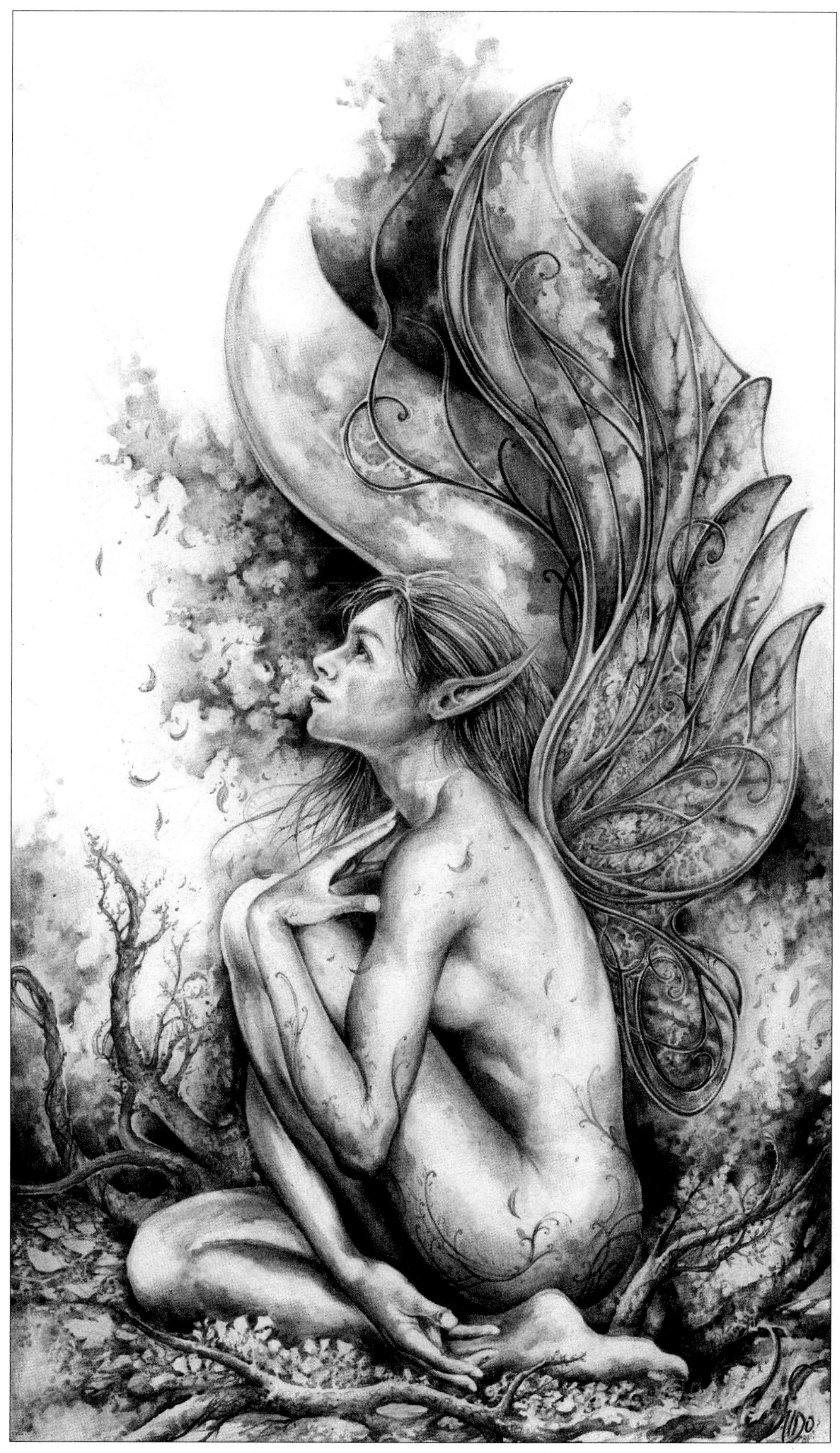

Aldo Perez

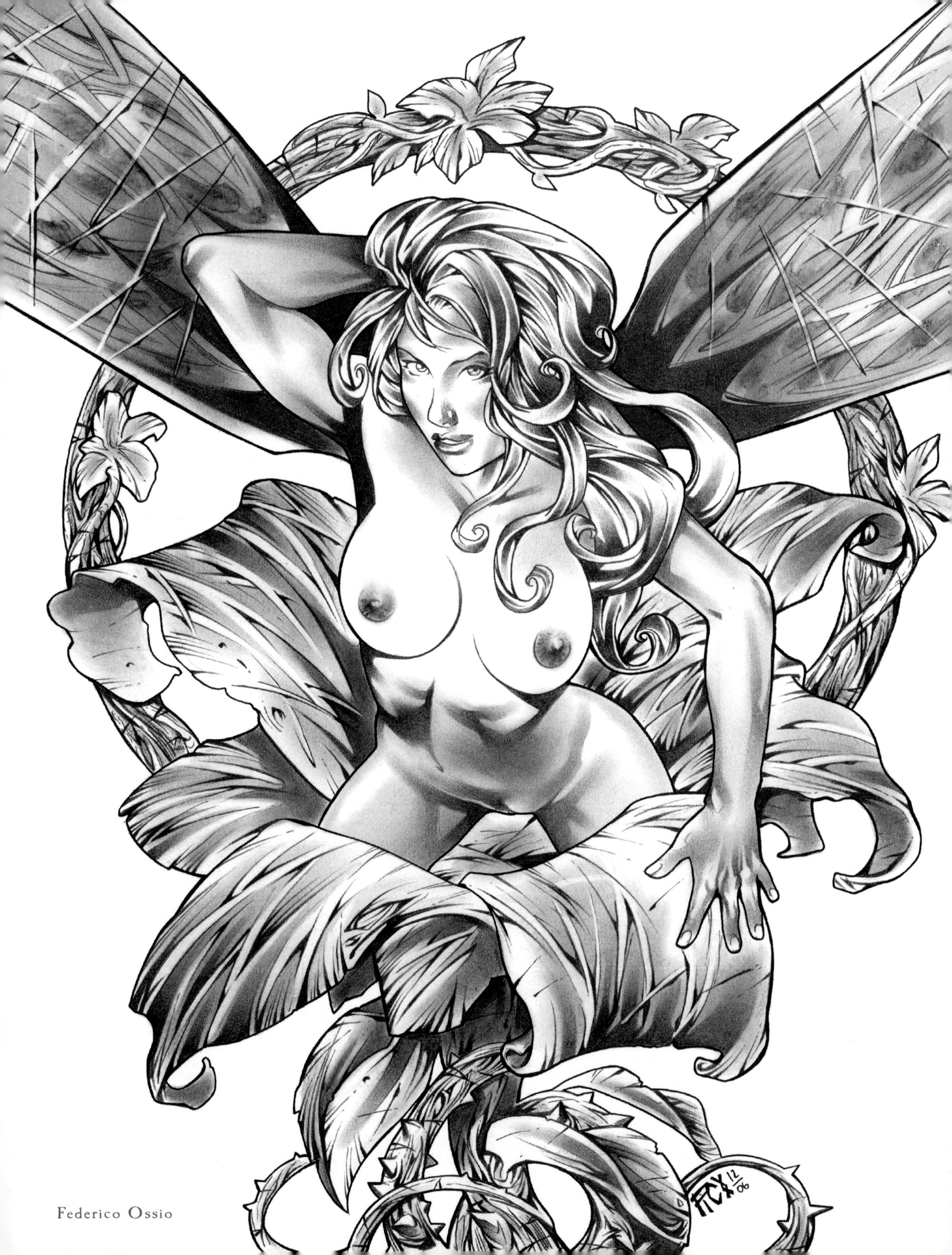

Federico Ossio

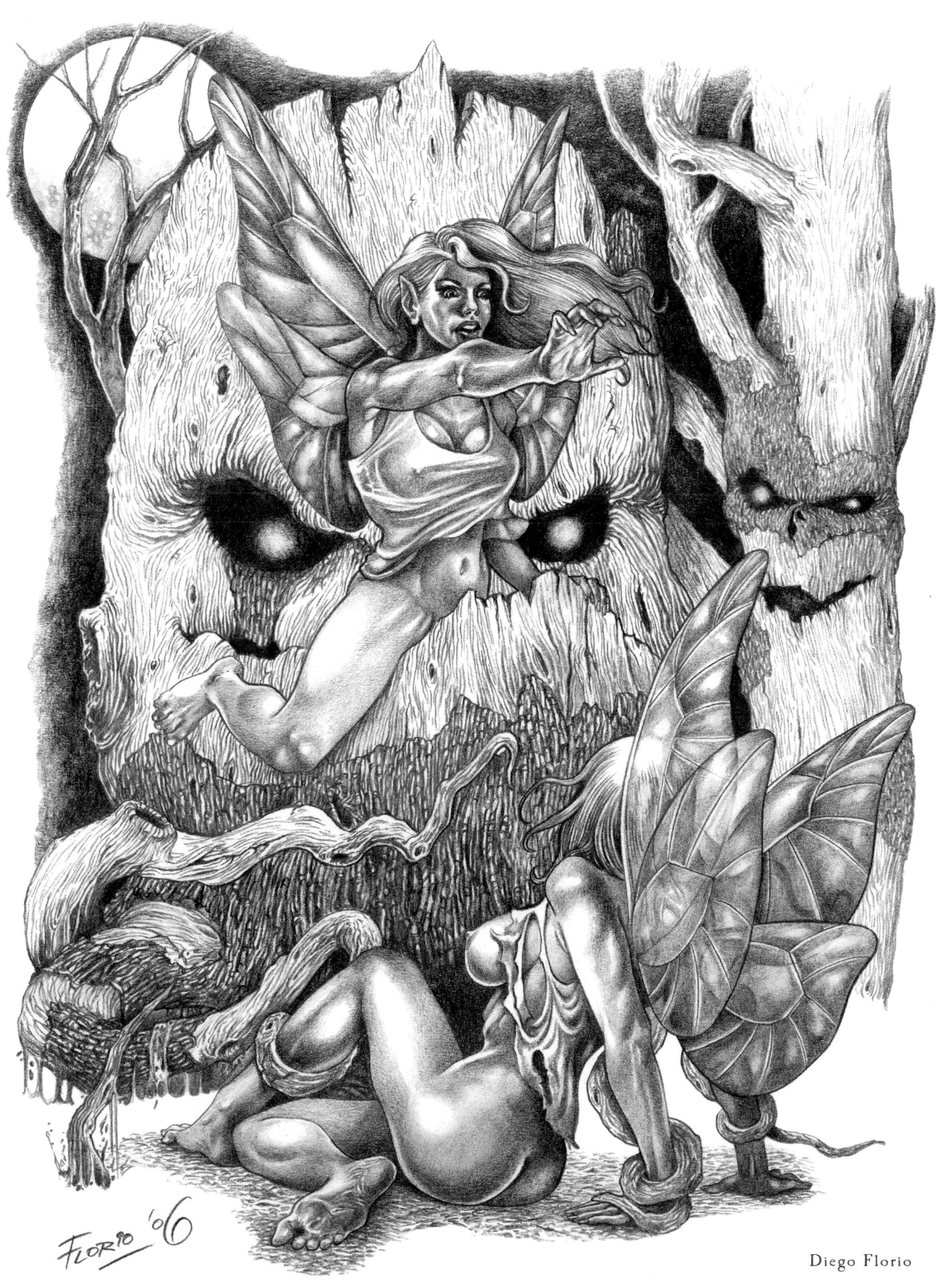

Diego Florio

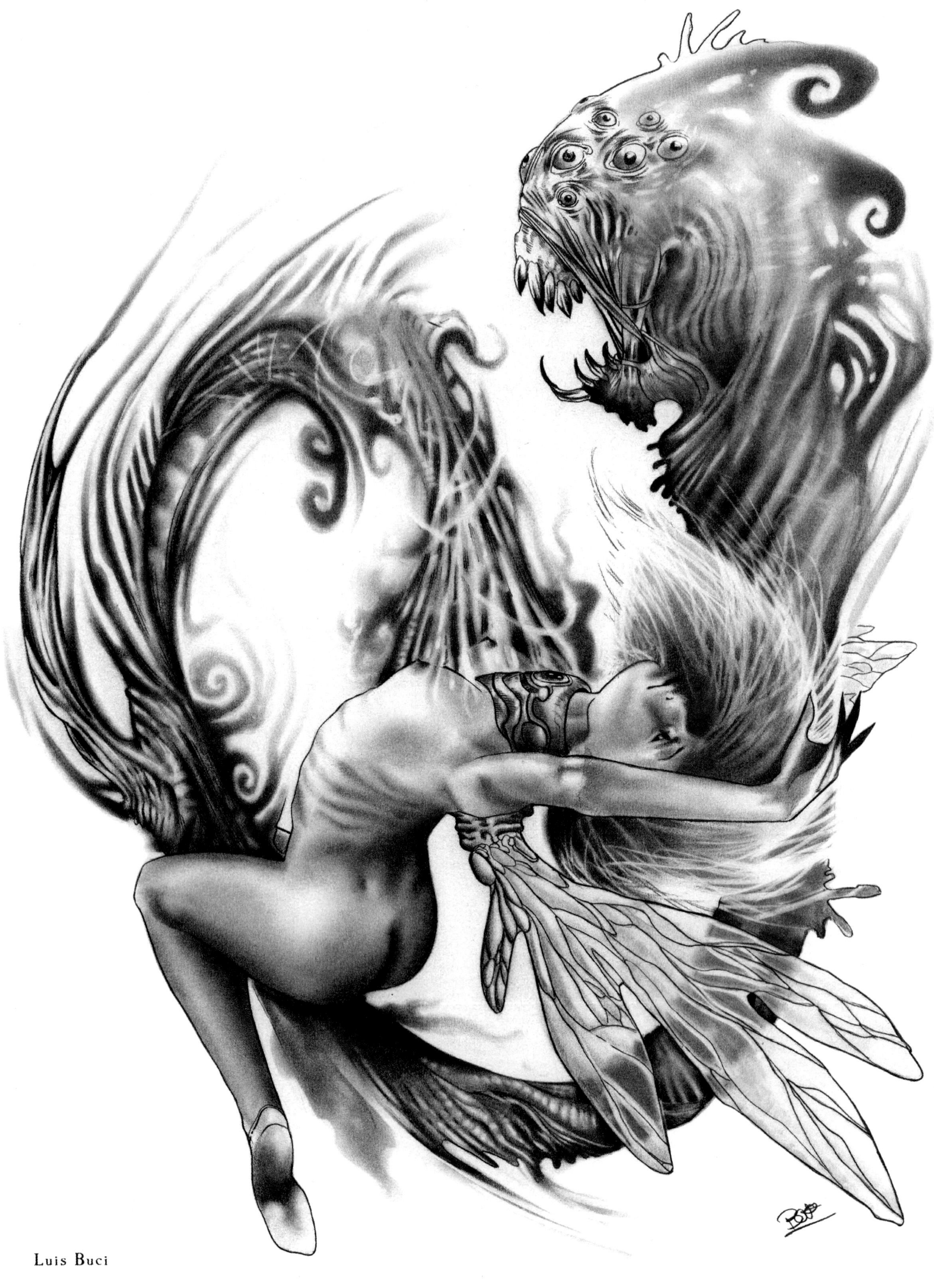

Luis Buci

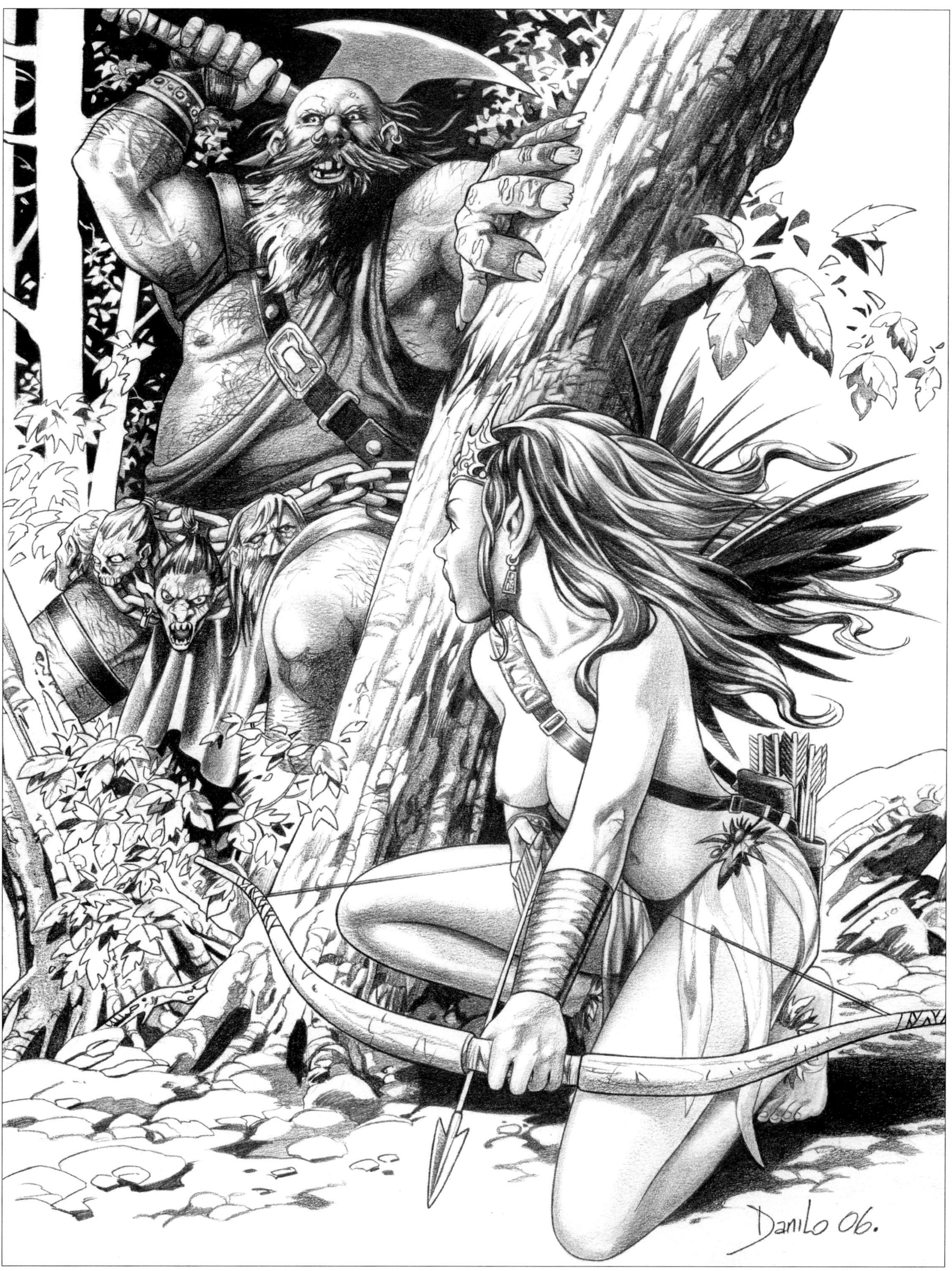

Danilo Guida

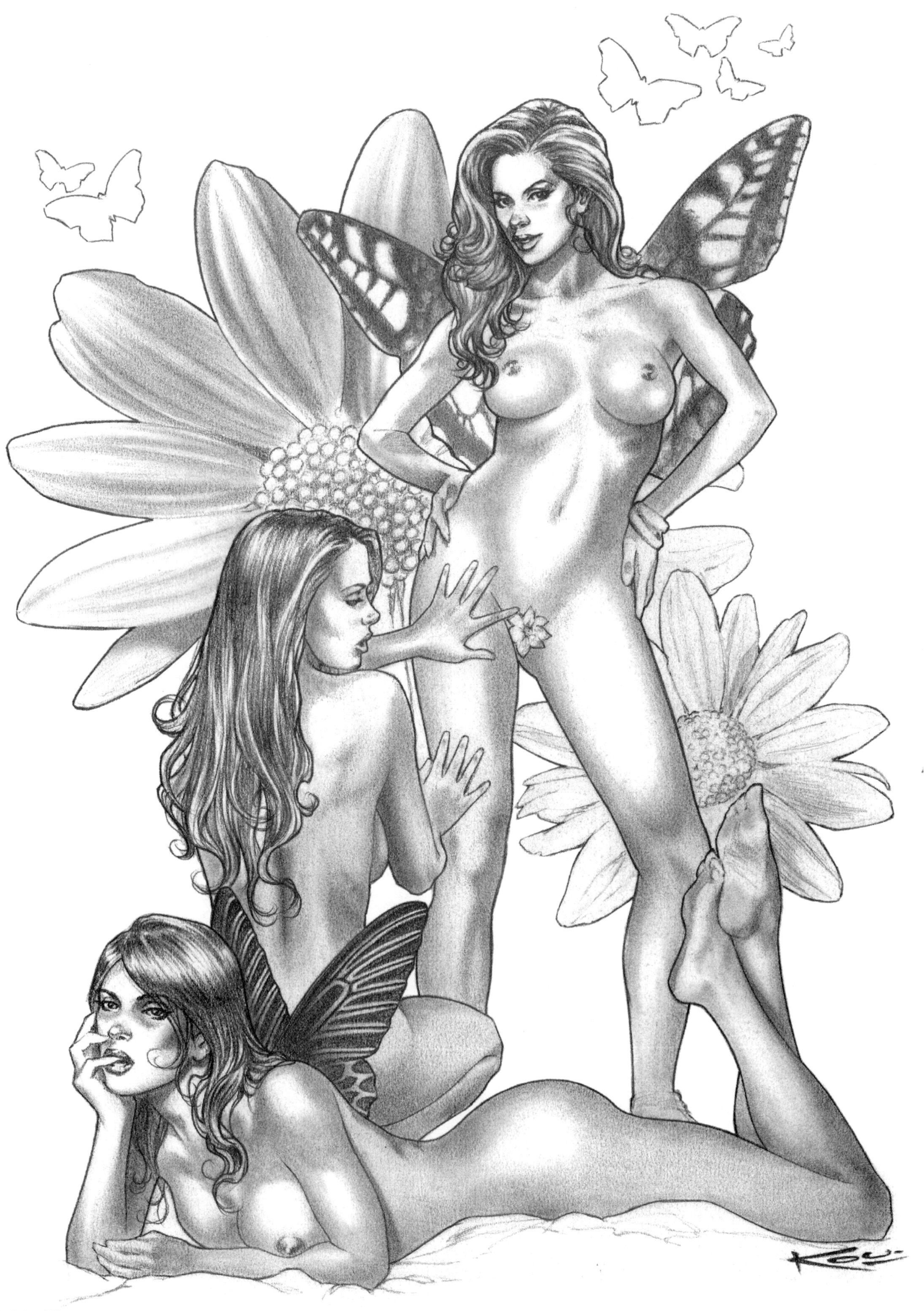

Pablo Kousovitis

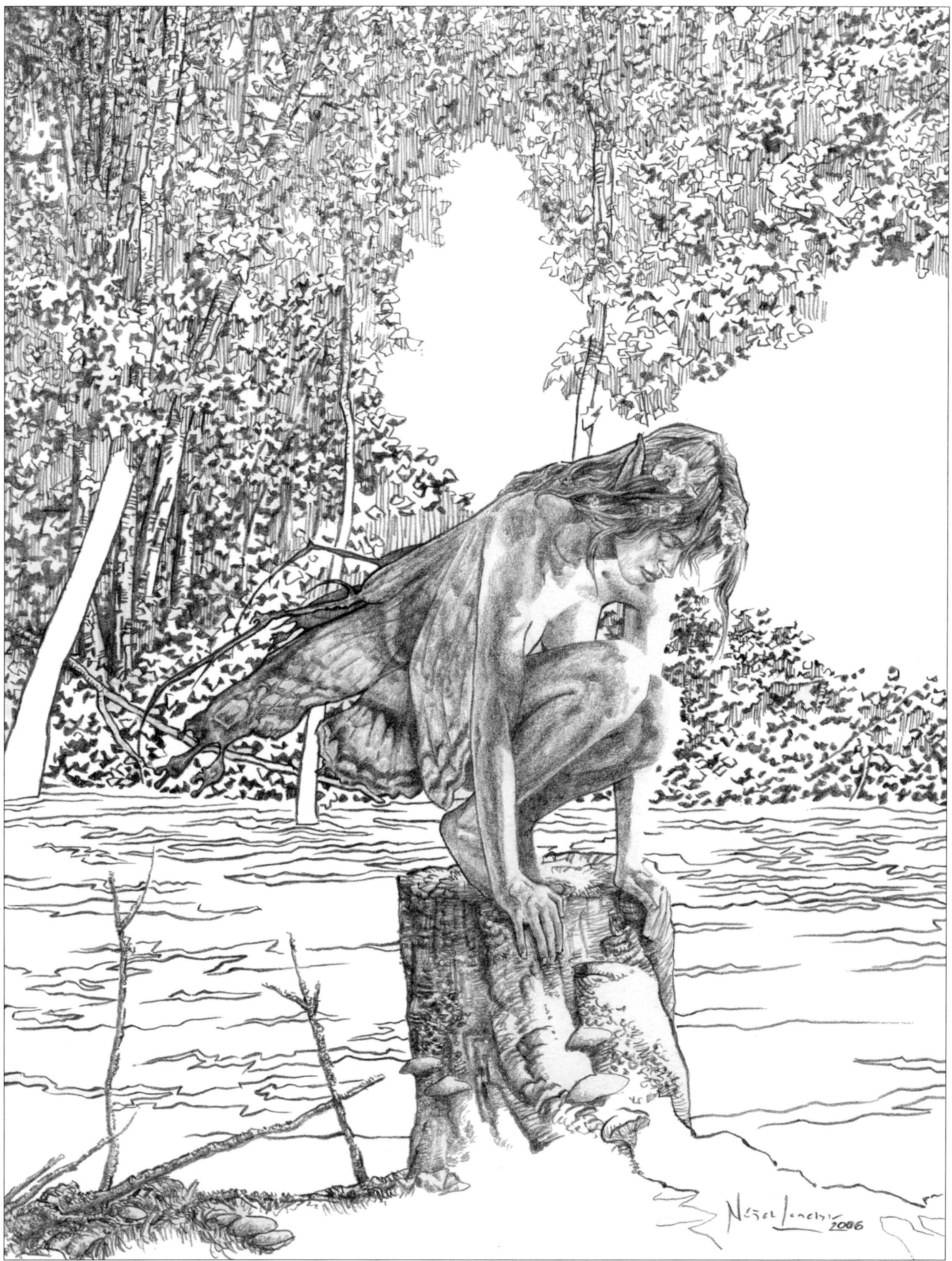

Juan Lencina

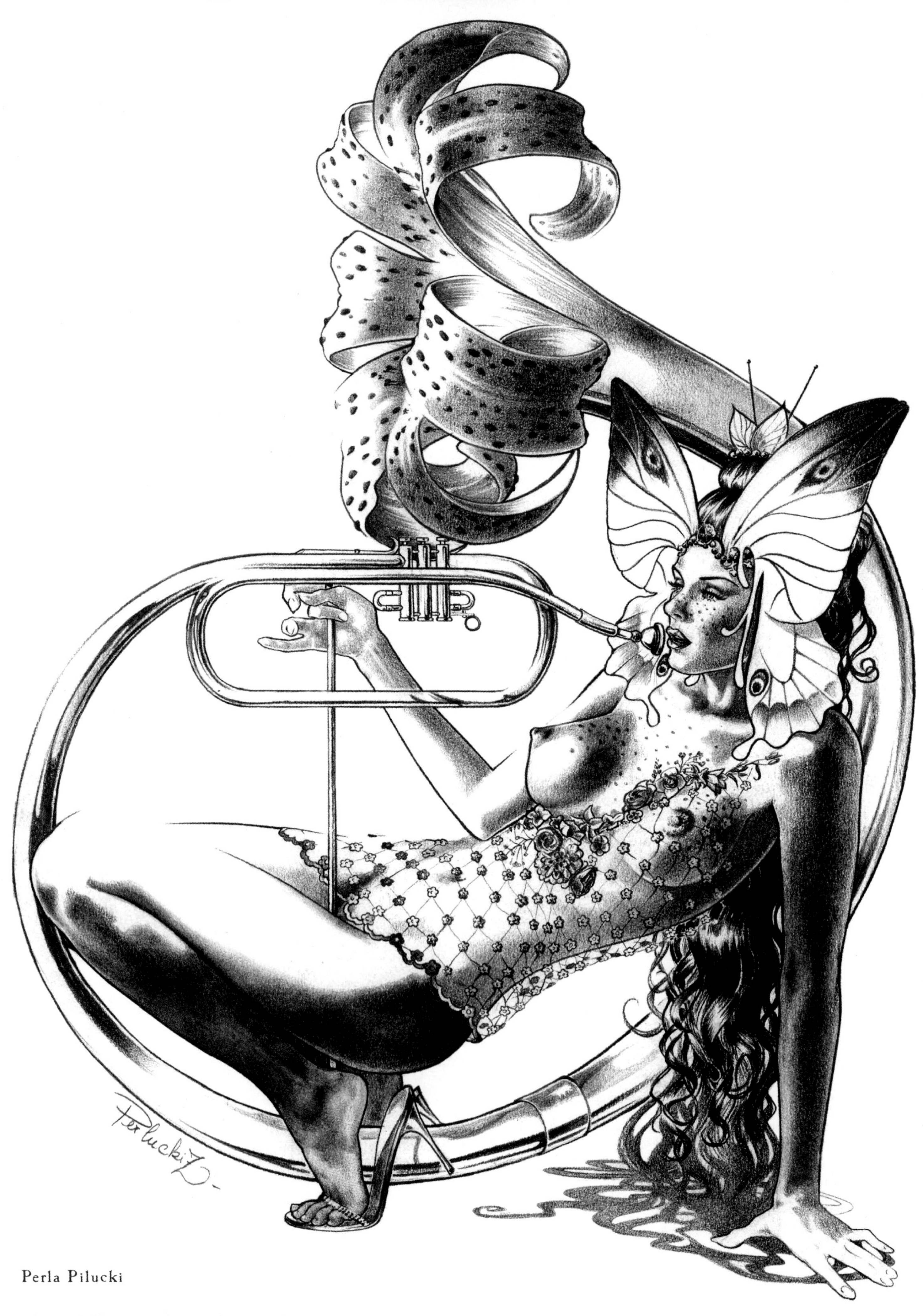

Perla Pilucki

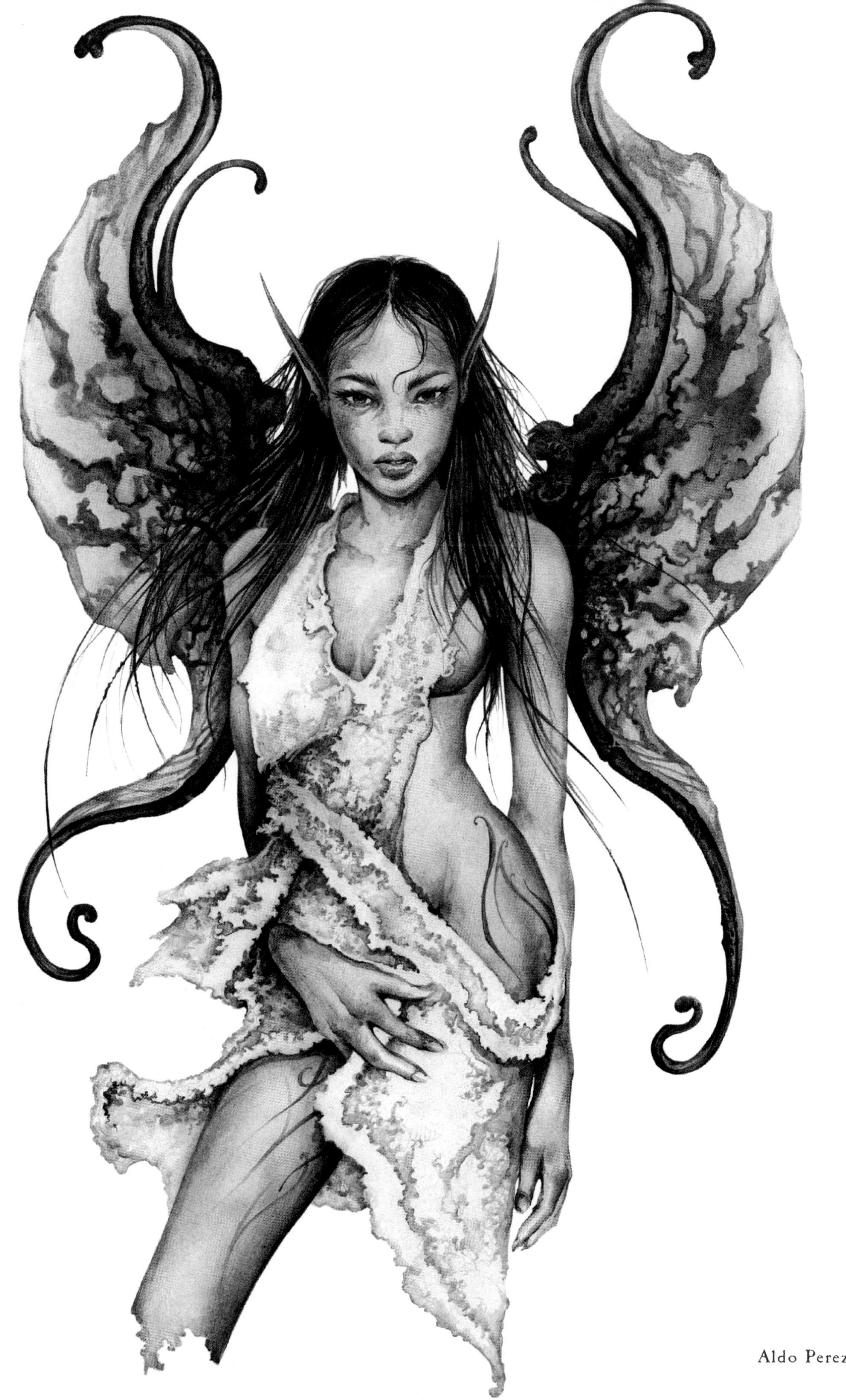

Aldo Perez

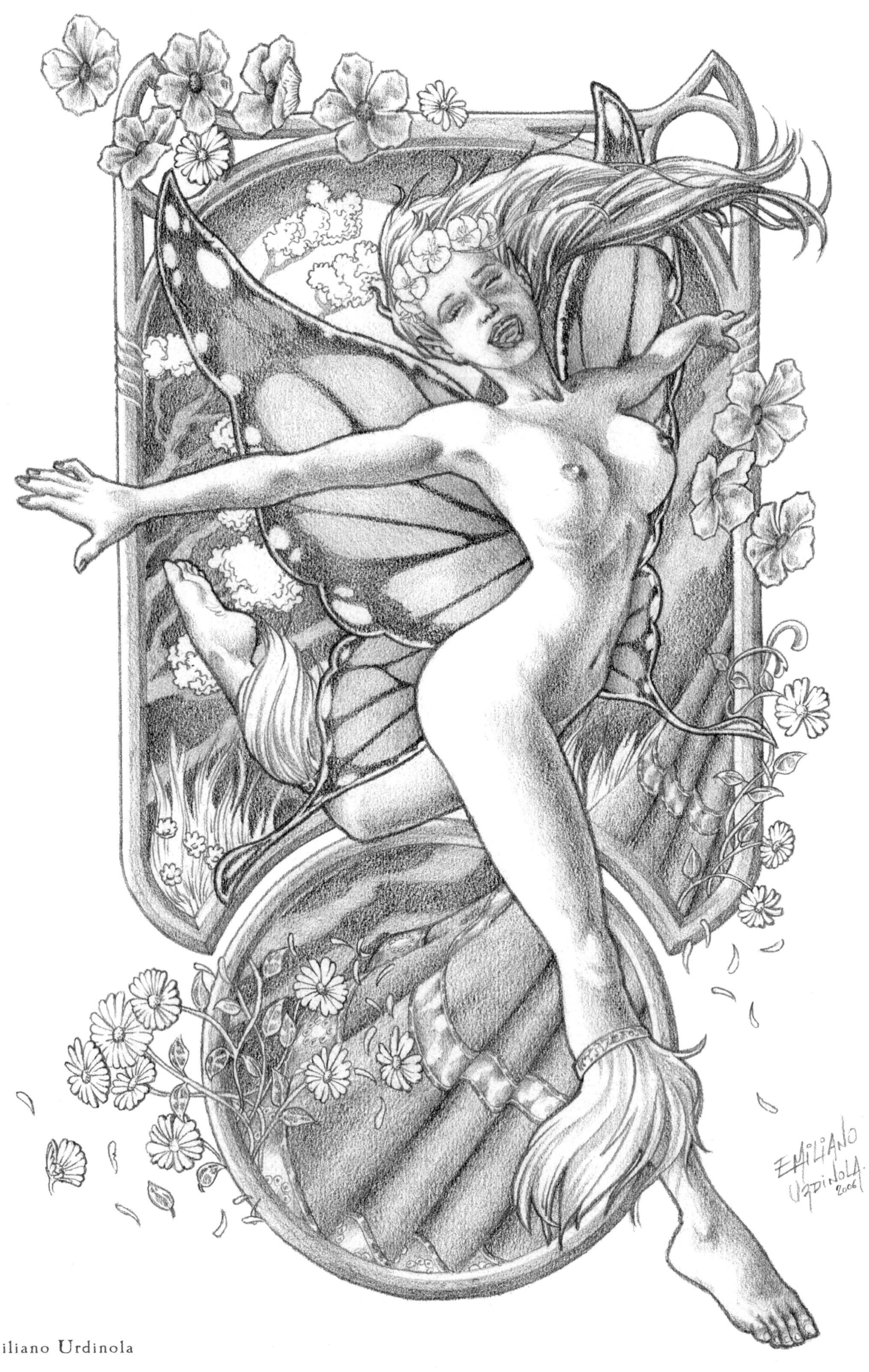

Emiliano Urdinola

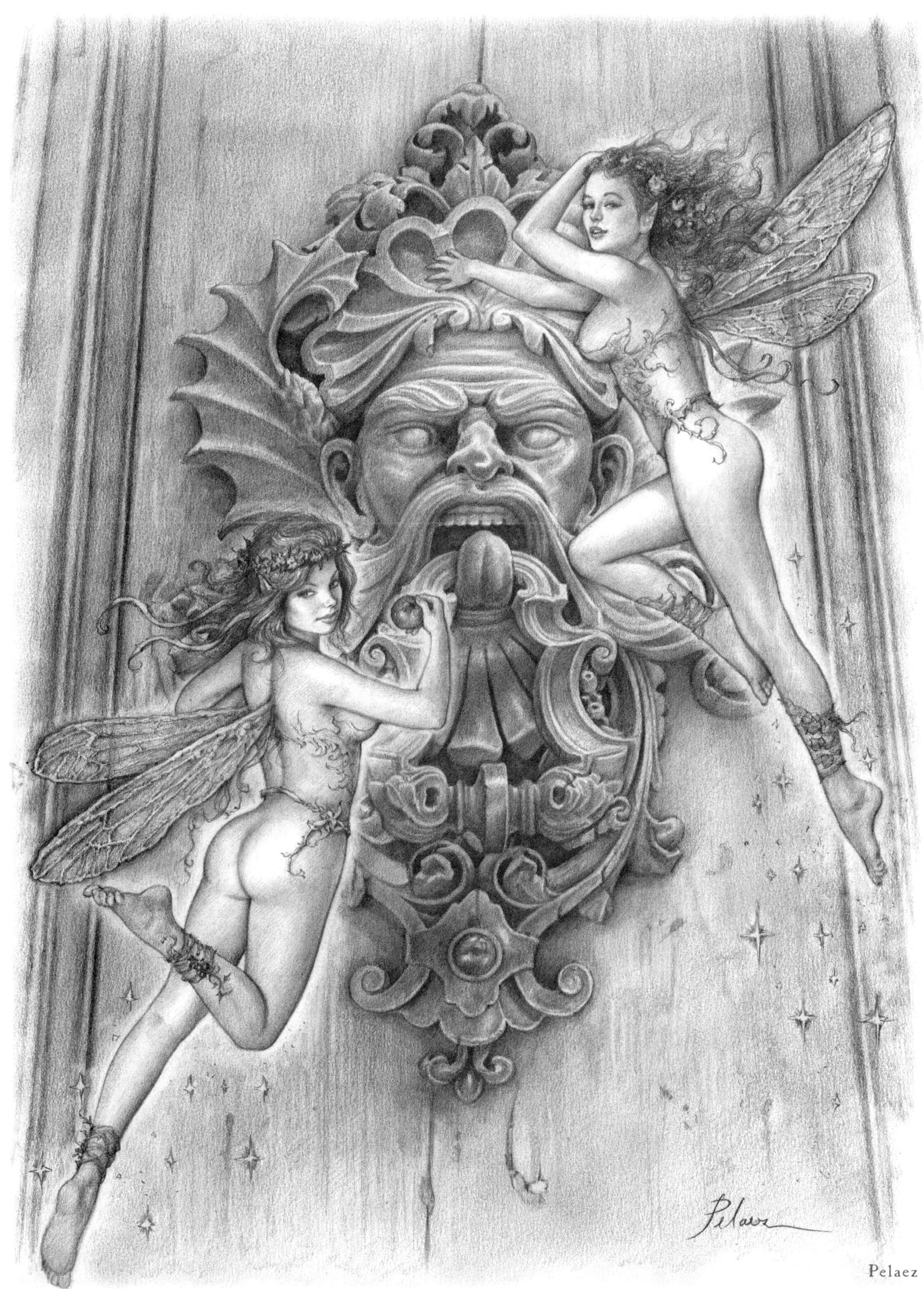

Pelaez

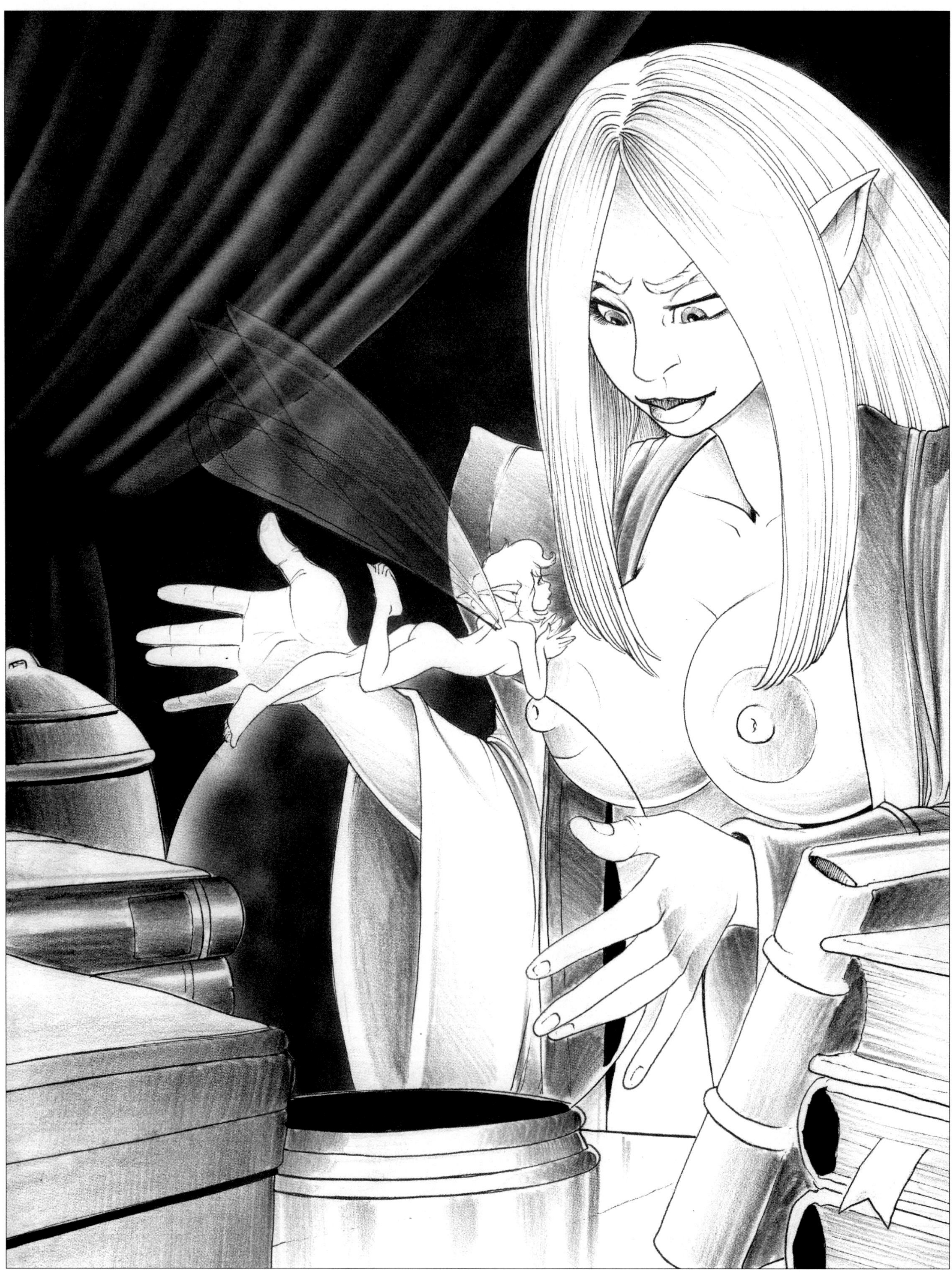

Barry Blair

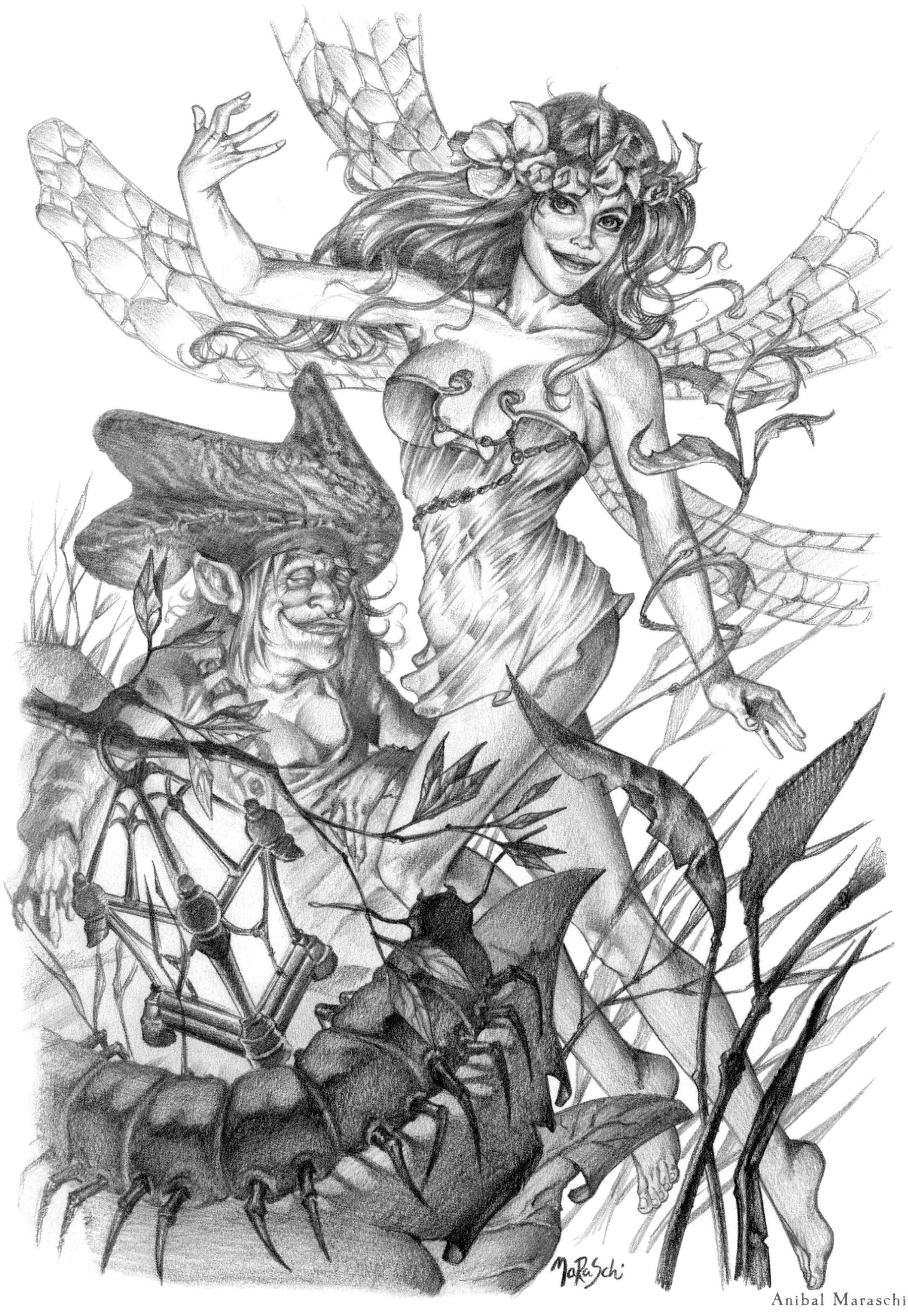

Anibal Maraschi

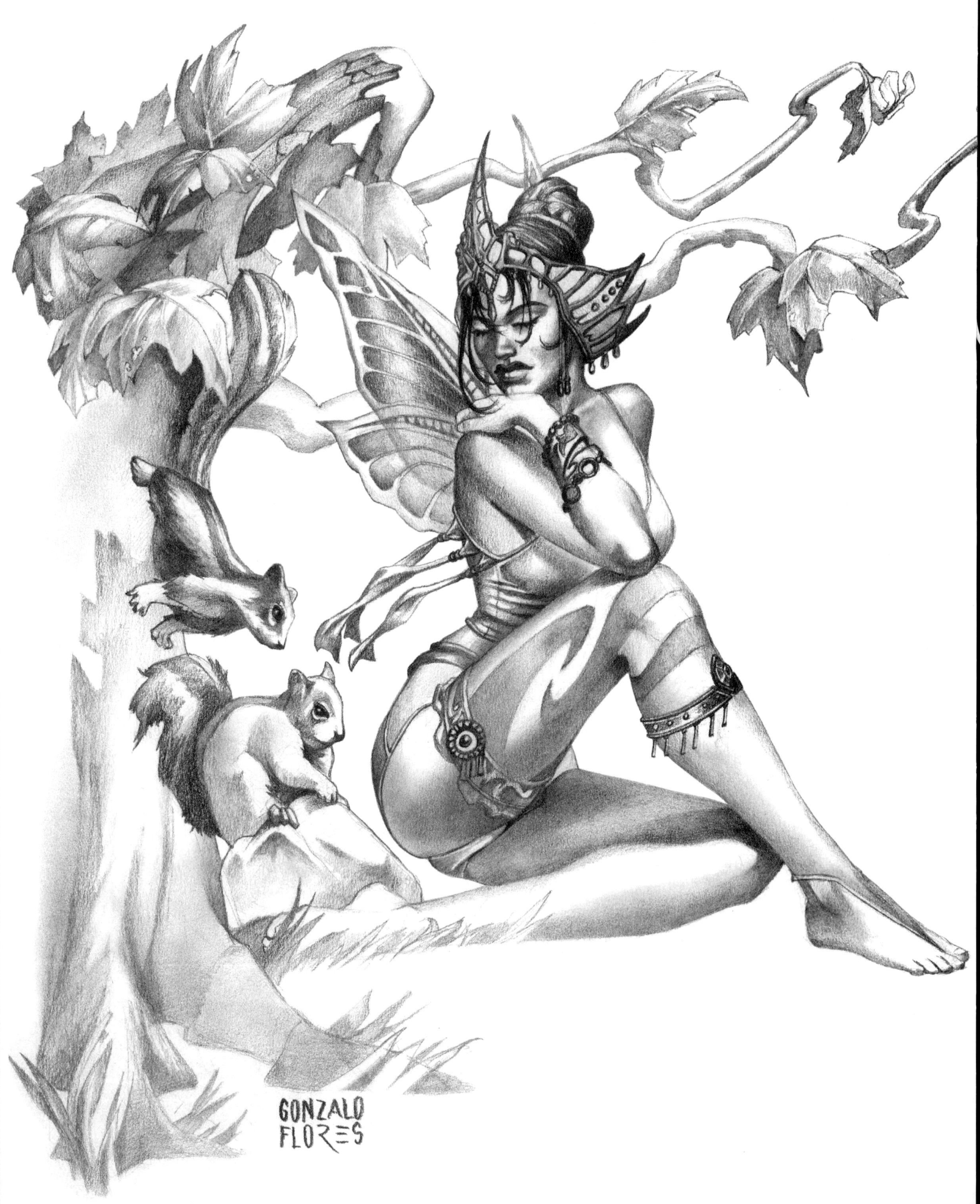

Gonzalo Flores

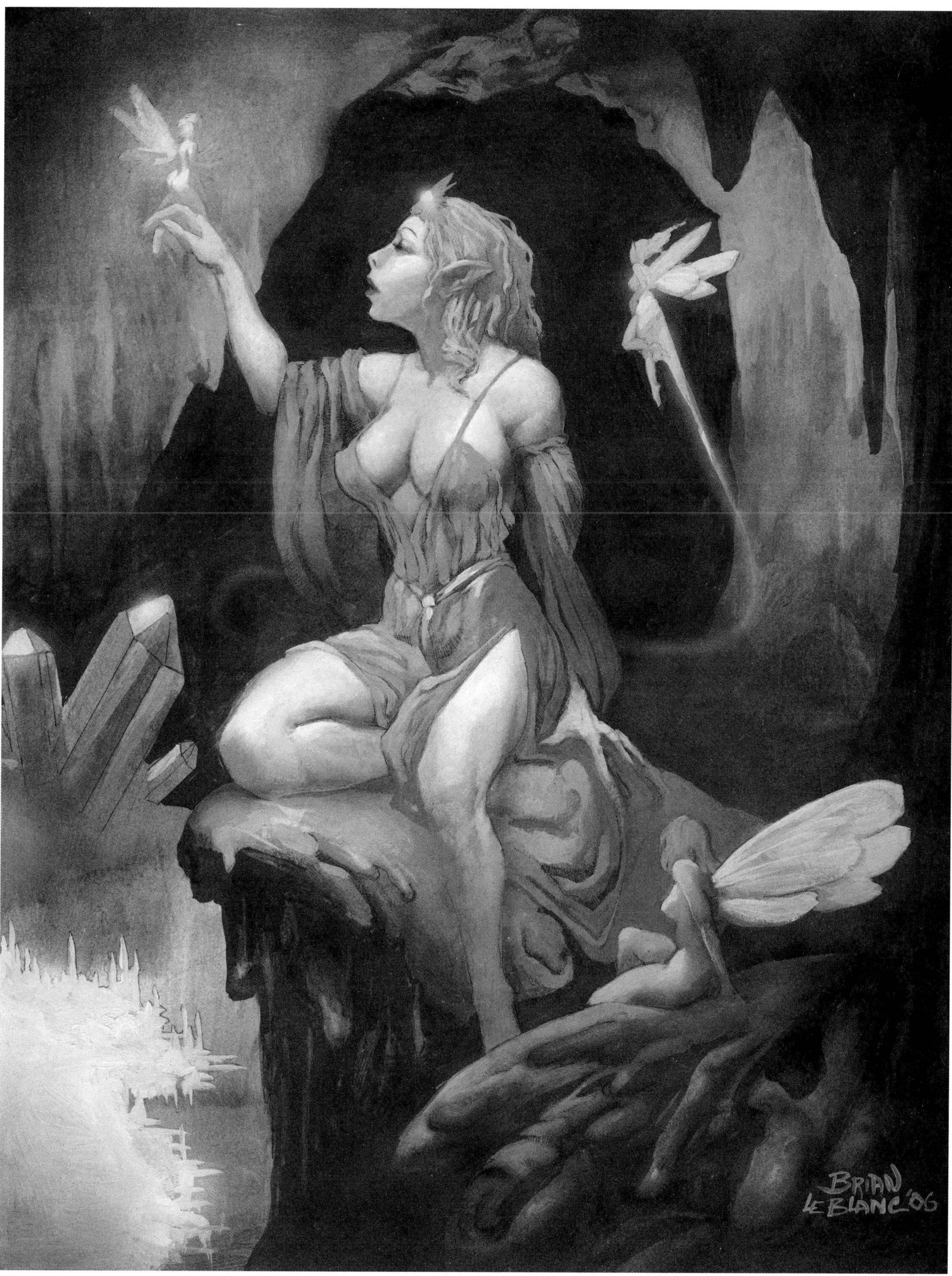

Brian LeBlanc

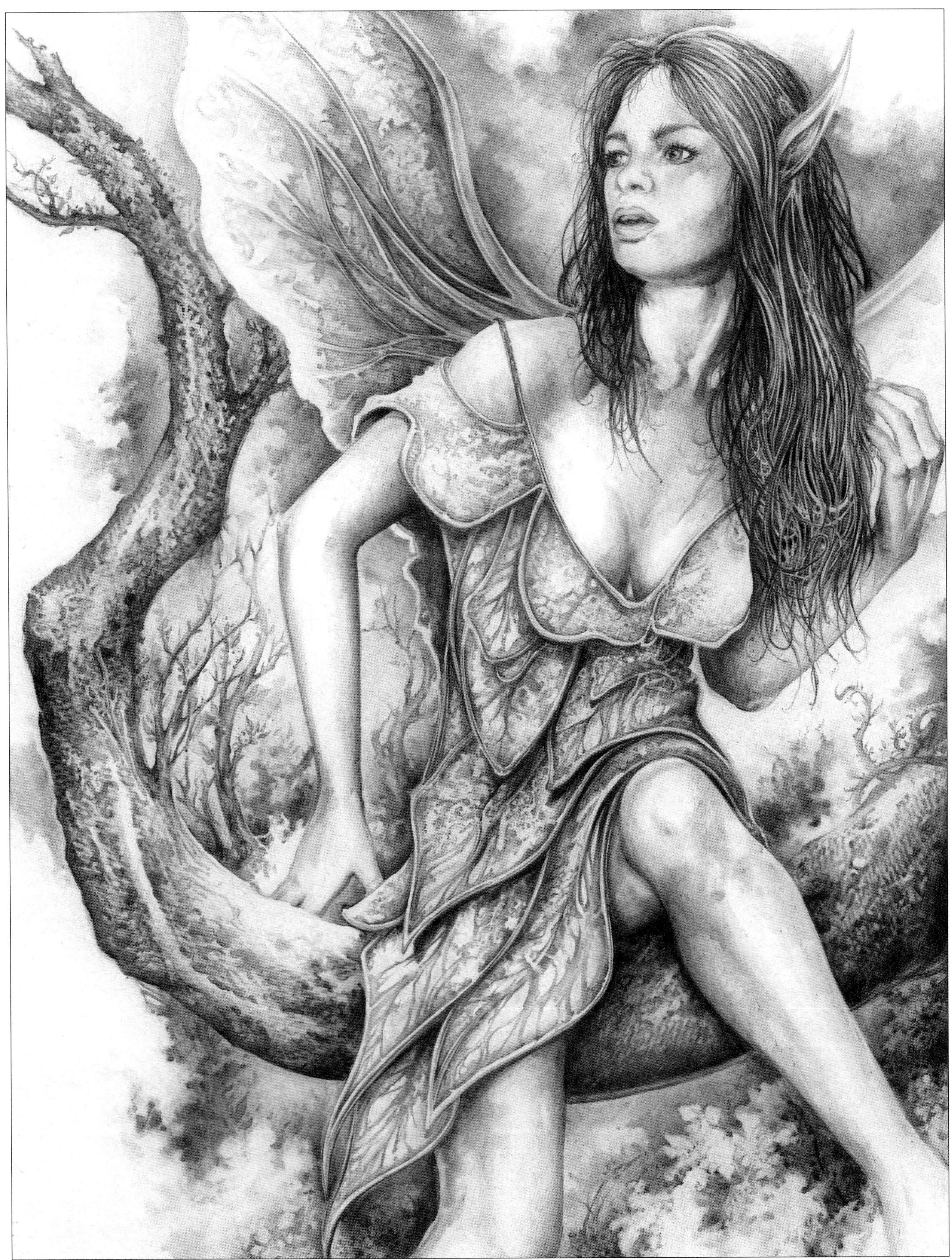

Aldo Perez

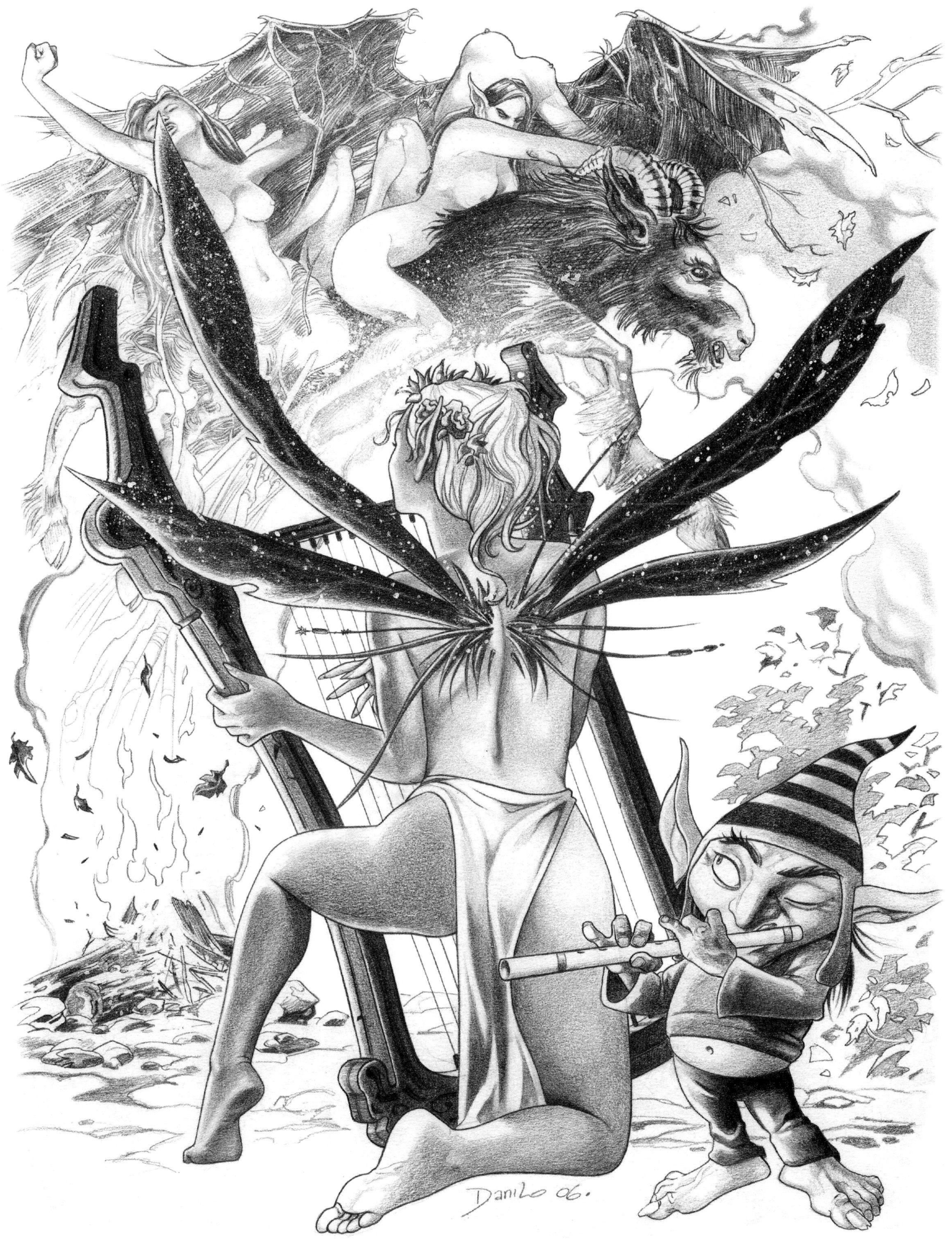

Danilo Guida

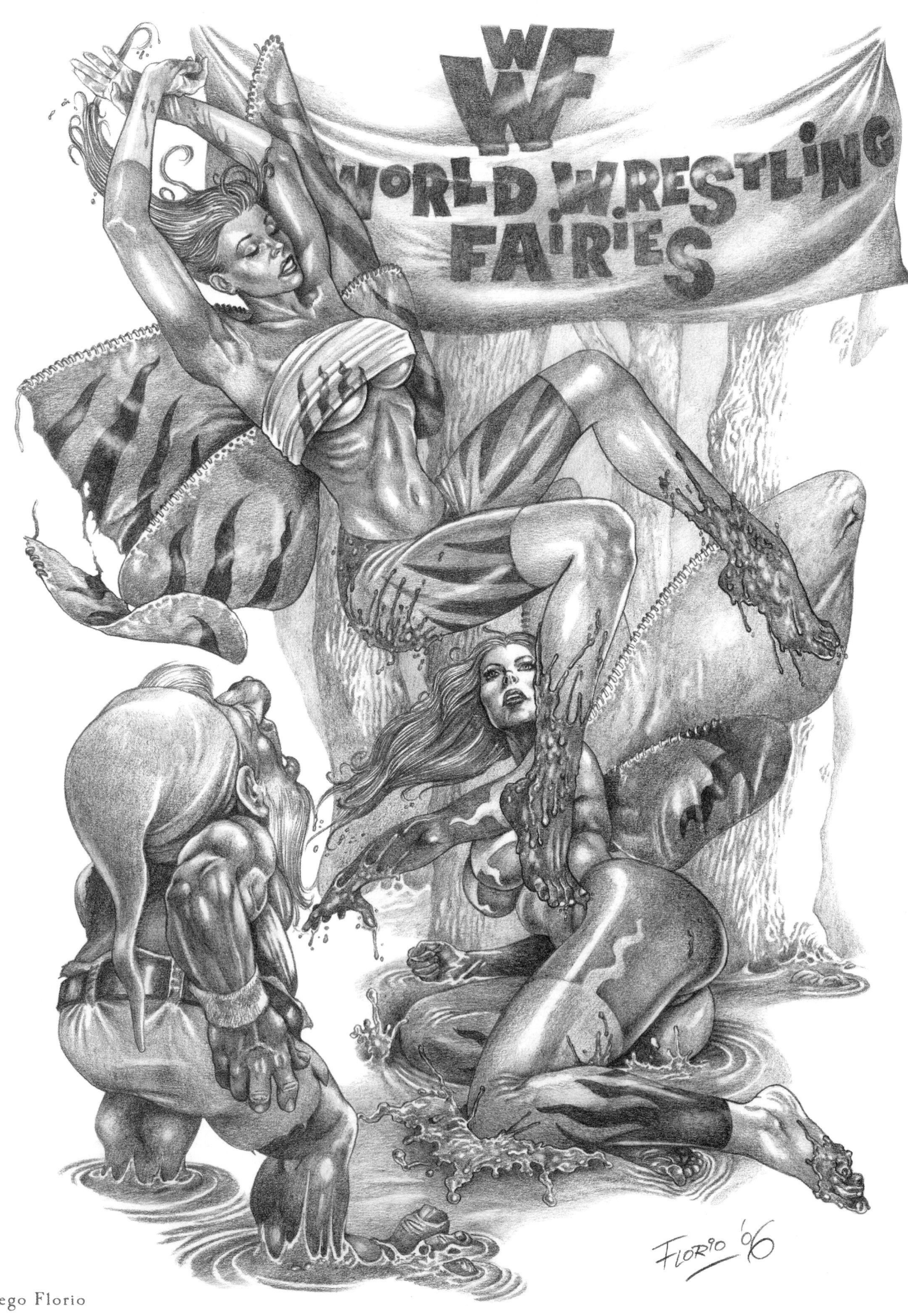

Diego Florio

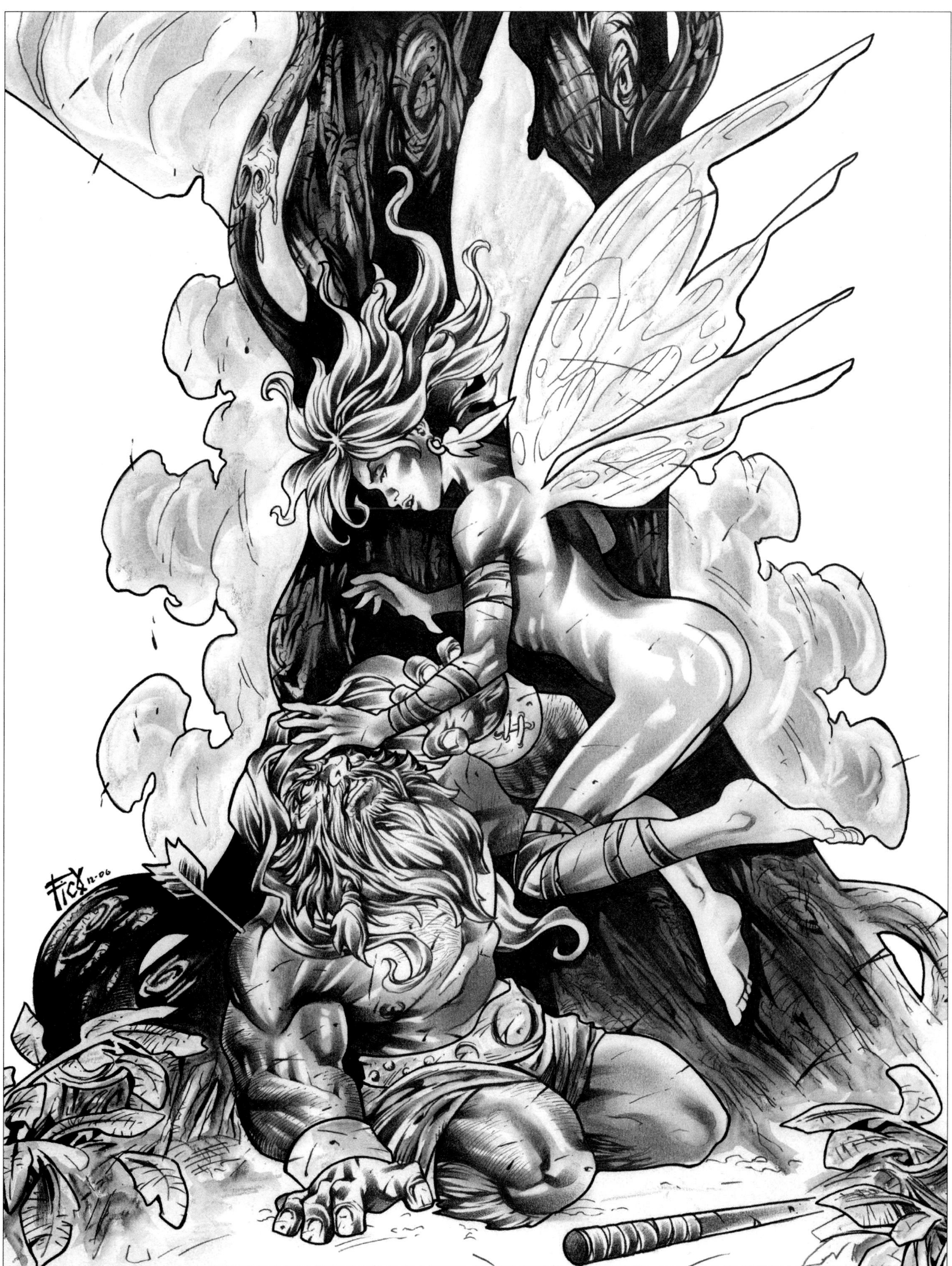

Federico Ossio

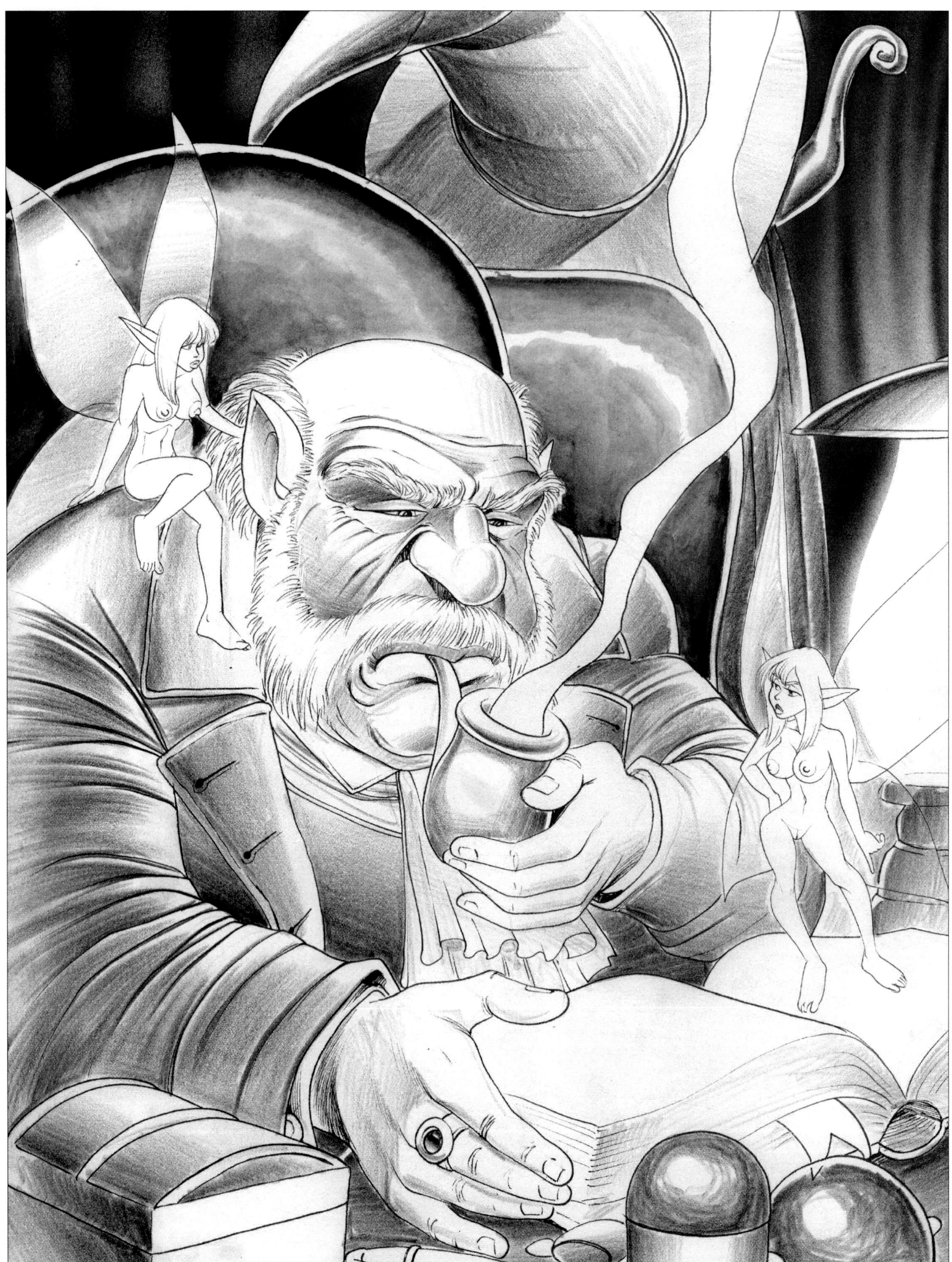

Barry Blair

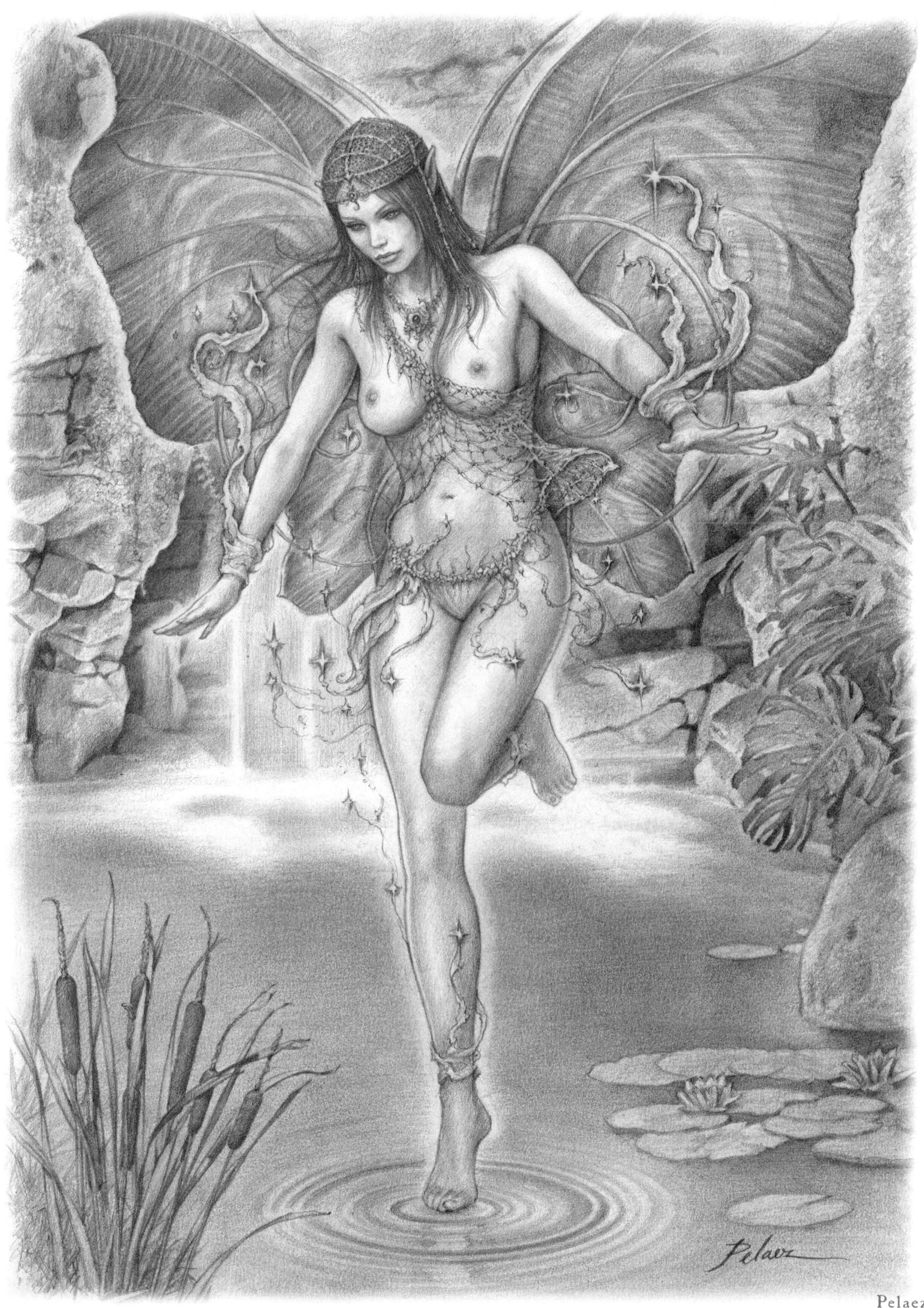

Pelaez

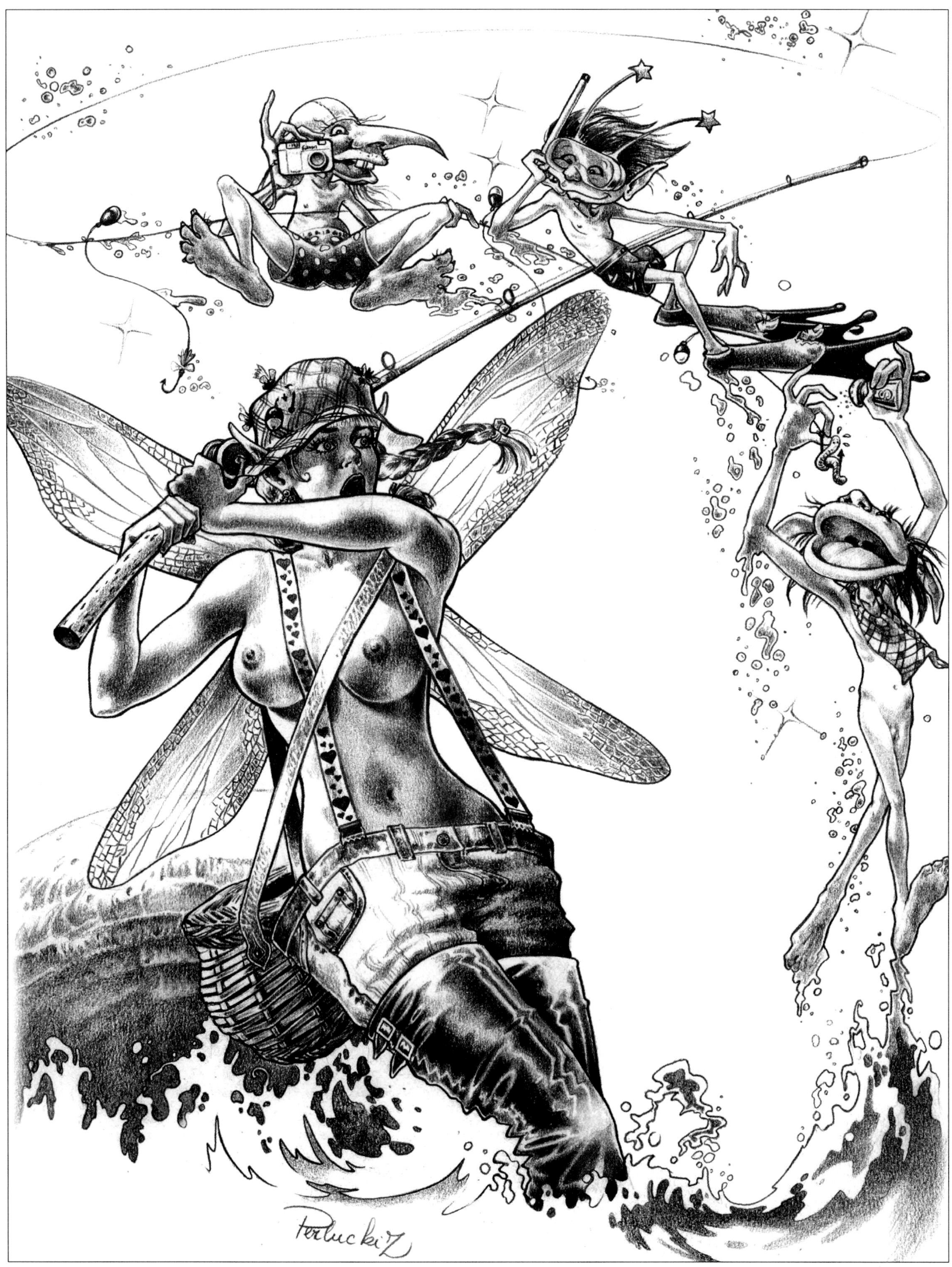

Perla Pilucki

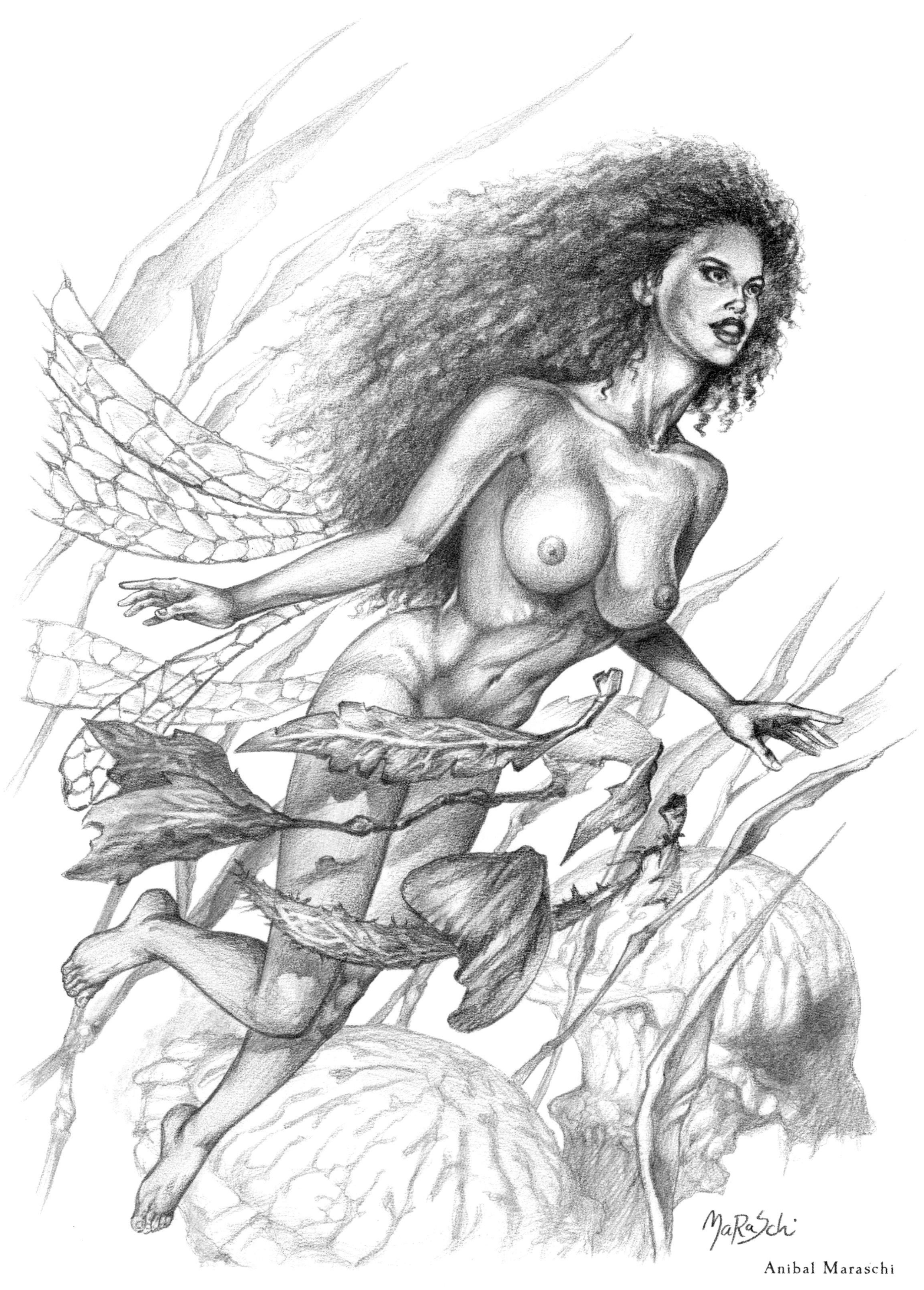

Anibal Maraschi

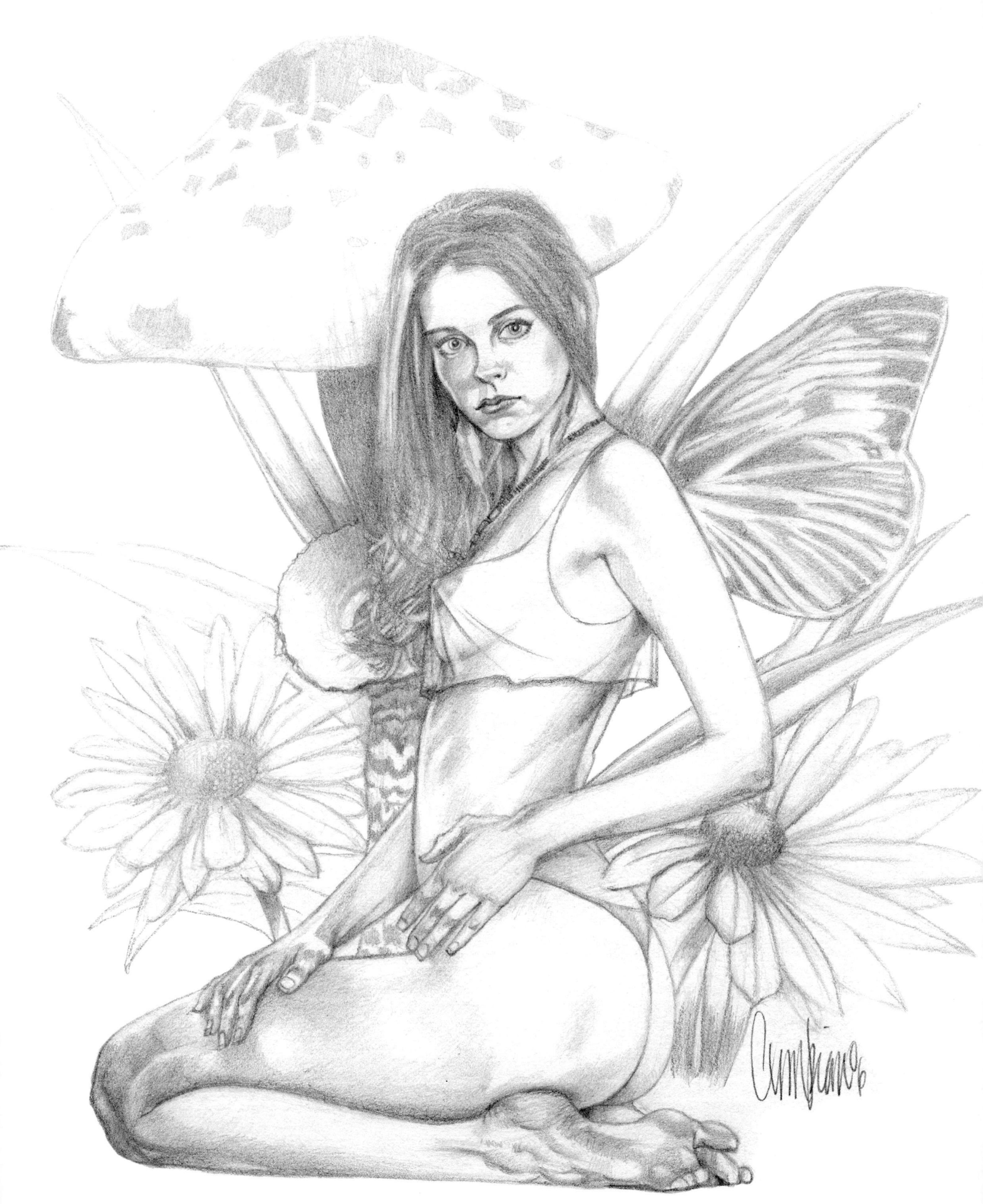

Ernesto Cumpian

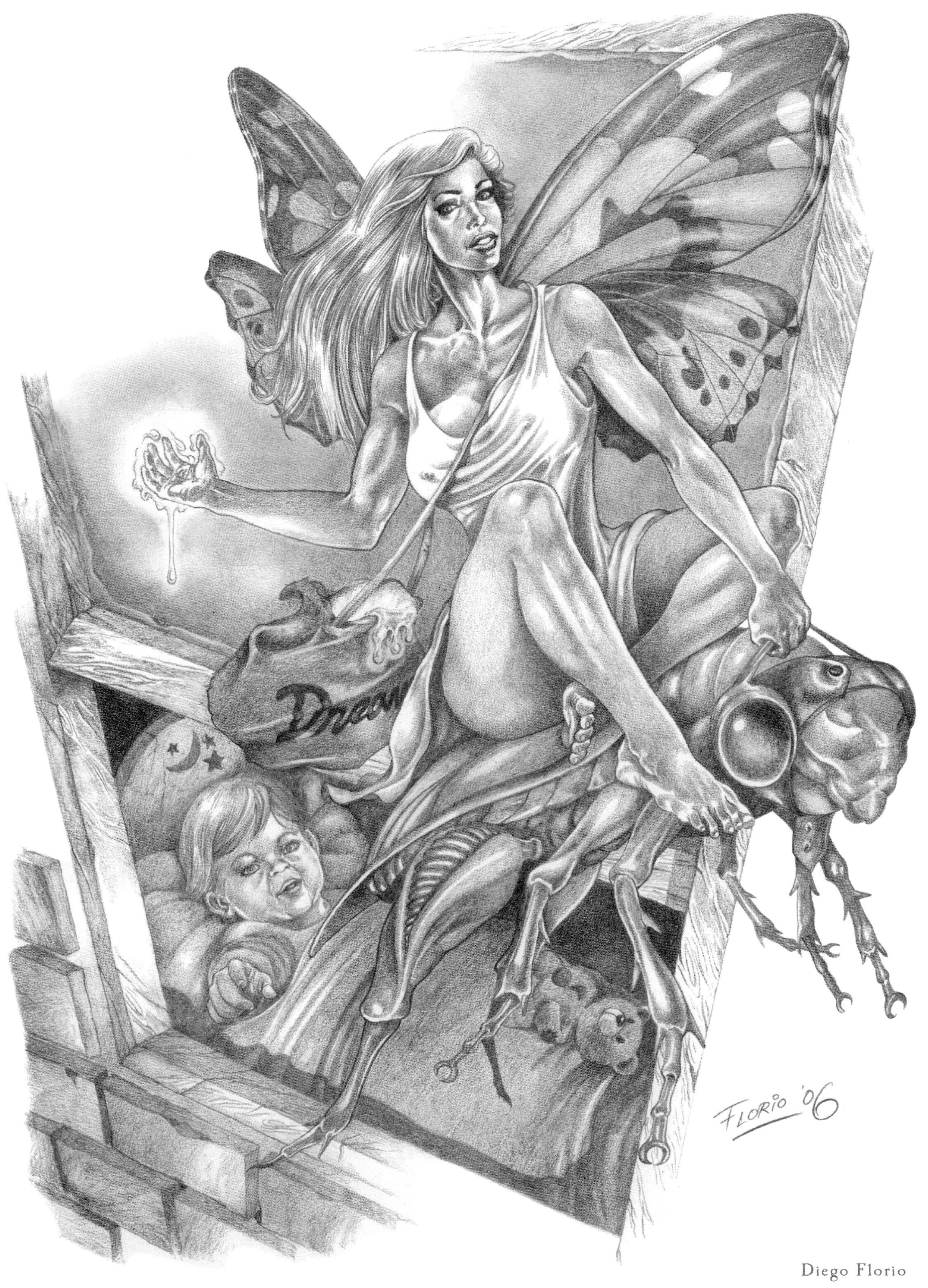

Diego Florio

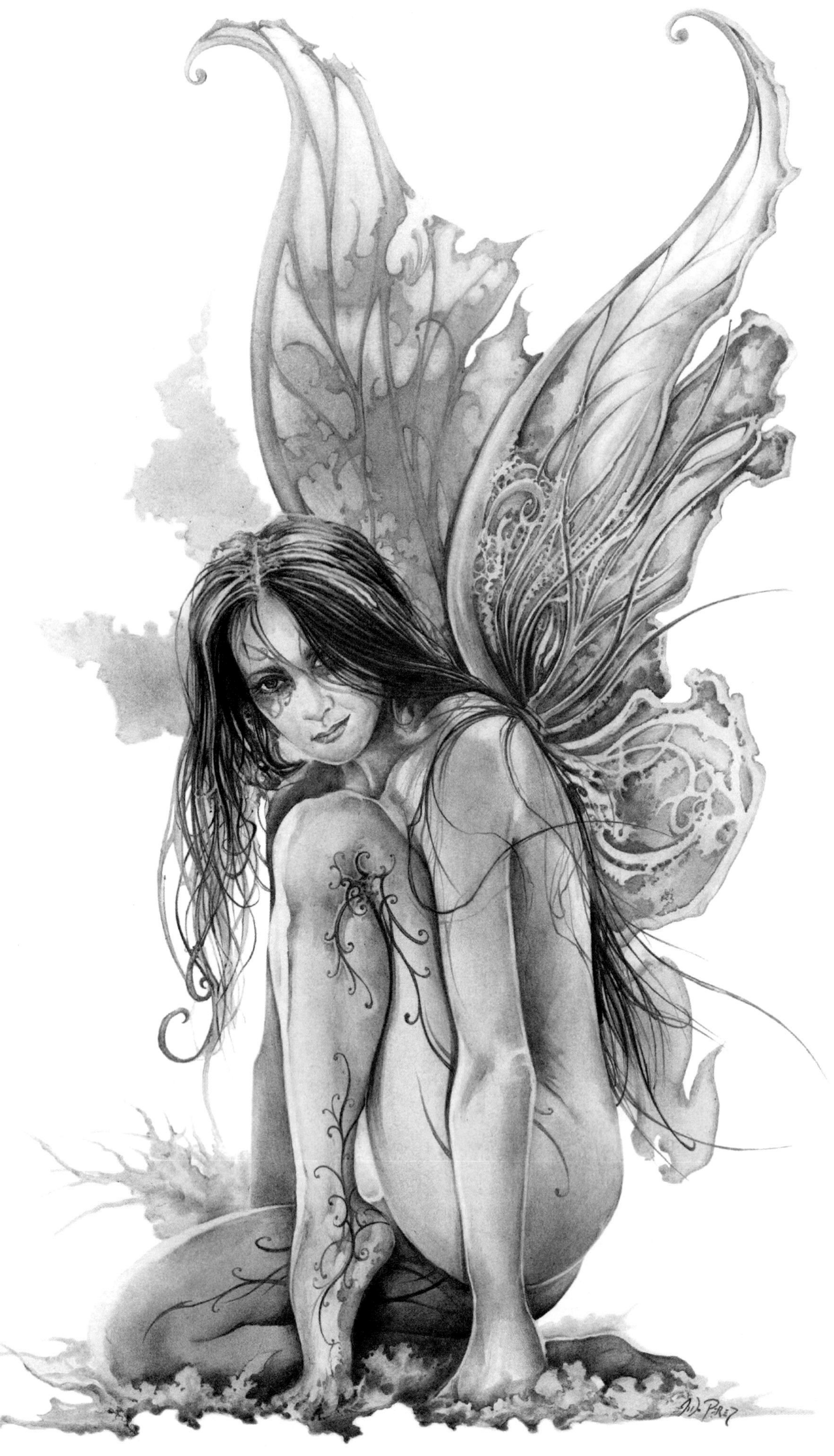

Aldo Perez

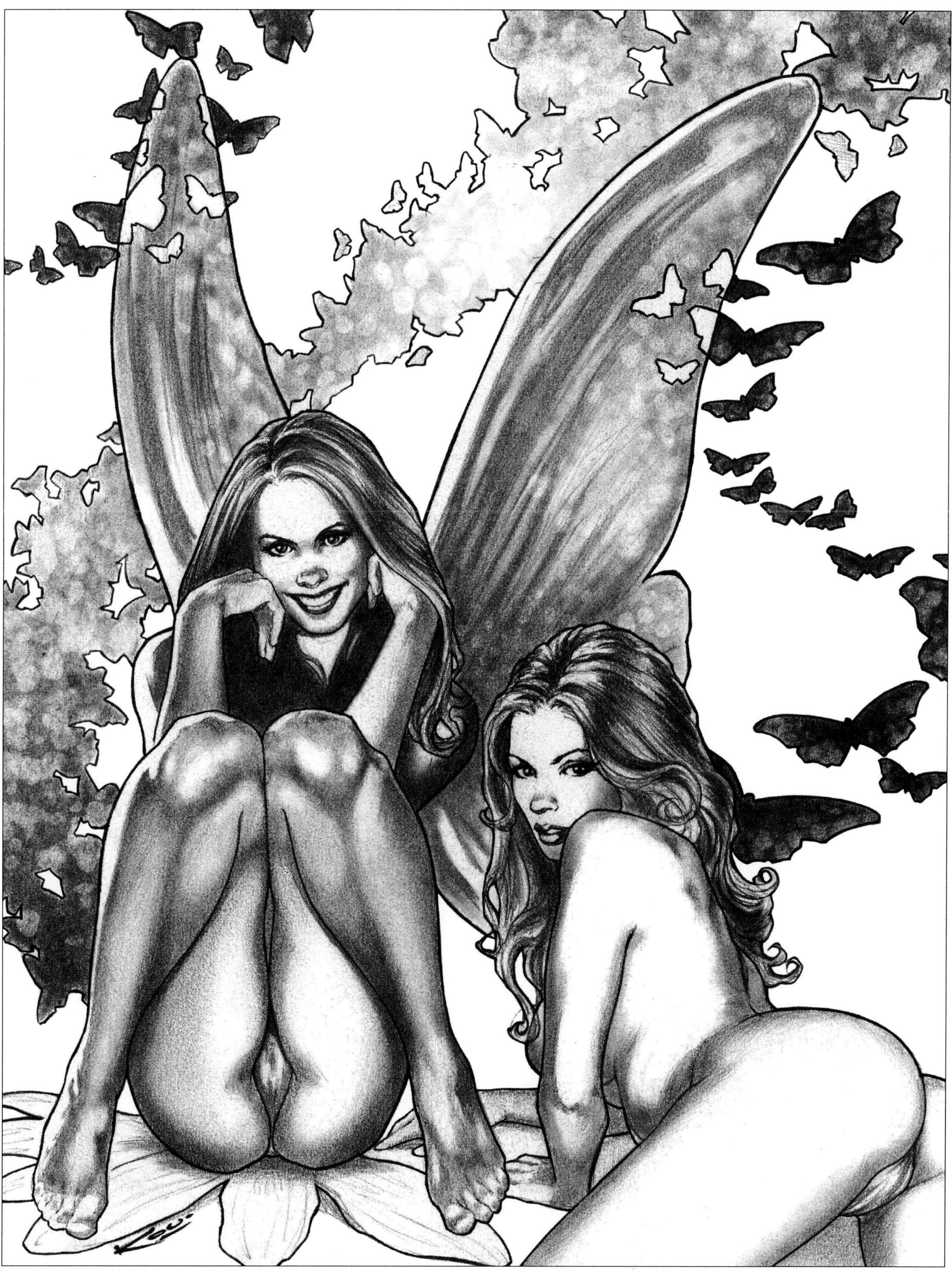

Pablo Kousovitis

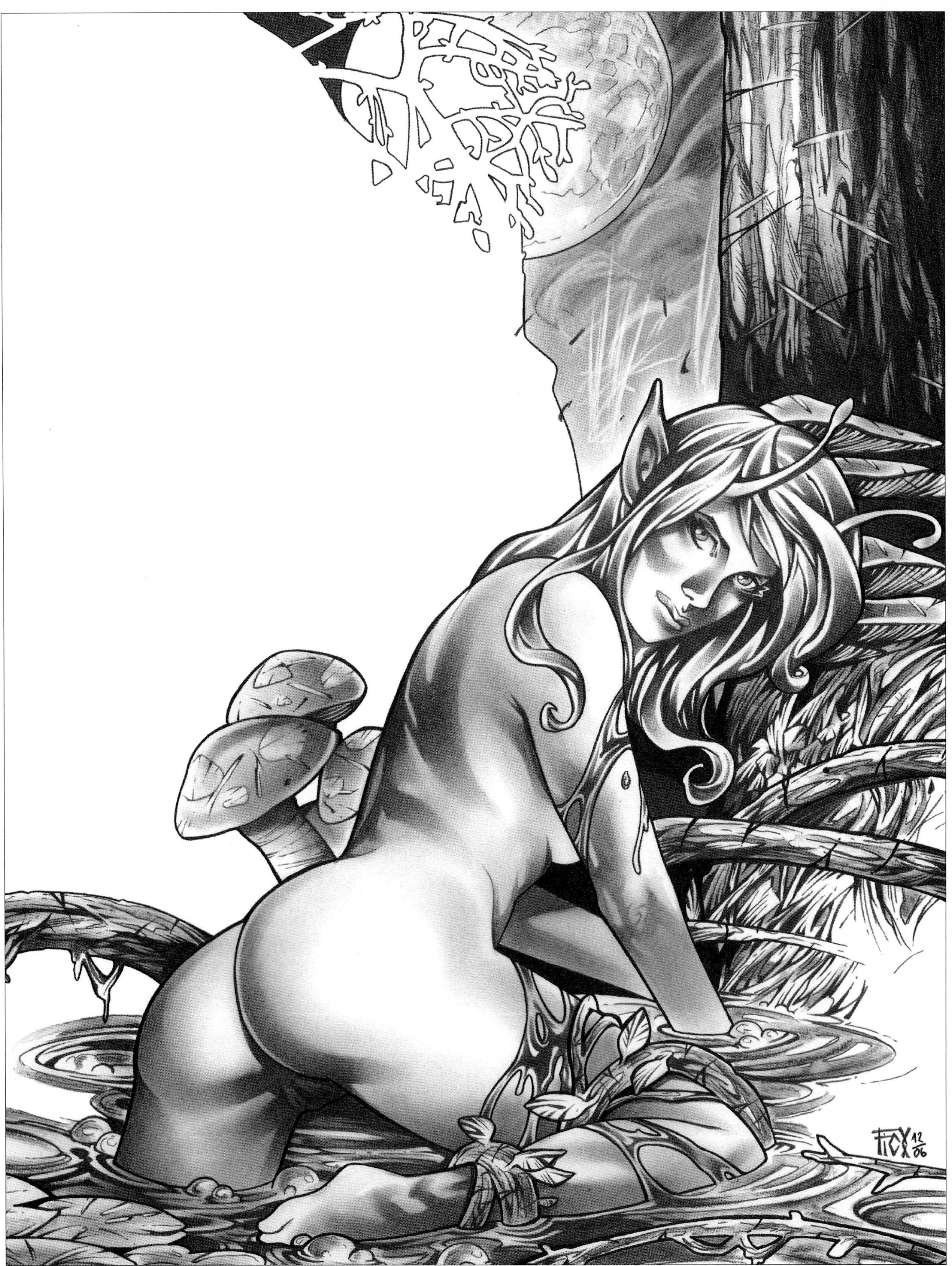

Federico Ossio